Heaton

from farms to foundries

Heaton Road, Newcastle.

Above, Heaton Road, around 1903 (see page 87).

Right, a Victorian collector's card for the East End Football Club. (P. Joannou-Newcastle United FC archive)

Previous page, Heaton Road about 1910.

Opposite, the Pavilion, Heaton Park, on a postcard postmarked 7 August 1907 ('Weather not too good, a glorious day tho' on Bank Holiday.'). Note the misspelling 'Henton Park' on the postcard.

Heaton

from farms to foundries

Henton Park, Newcastle on Tyne.

Alan Morgan

Tyne Bridge Publishing

Acknowledgements

The author and Tyne Bridge Publishing would like to thank the following for their generous help in the production of this book: John Allan, Paul Joannou, ncjMedia.

Information gleaned from the publications of the following was invaluable: Brian Bennison *Heavy Nights*, Frank Manders *Cinemas of Newcastle*, Lynn Pearson *The Northumbrian Pub*, Jordan Tinniswood *Before They Were United*, Les Turnbull *Coals from Newcastle*, N. Moore and W.K. Robinson *Heaton Methodist Church*.

Illustrations

Maps, photographs and drawings in this book are reproduced from the Heritage Collection at Newcastle Libraries, unless otherwise indicated.

Front cover, Heaton Road around 1903.
Back cover, back Heaton Park Road and Molineux Street, 1914; East End FC card (P. Joannou-Newcastle United FC archive)
Right, Heaton Road, 1972.
Page 5, Fifth Avenue, 1969.

©Alan Morgan, 2012
Published by
City of Newcastle upon Tyne
Newcastle Libraries & Information Service
Tyne Bridge Publishing, 2012

www.tynebridgepublishing.co.uk
www.newcastle.gov.uk/libraries

ISBN: 978-1-857952-06-3

Printed by Elanders UK Ltd., North Tyneside

Contents

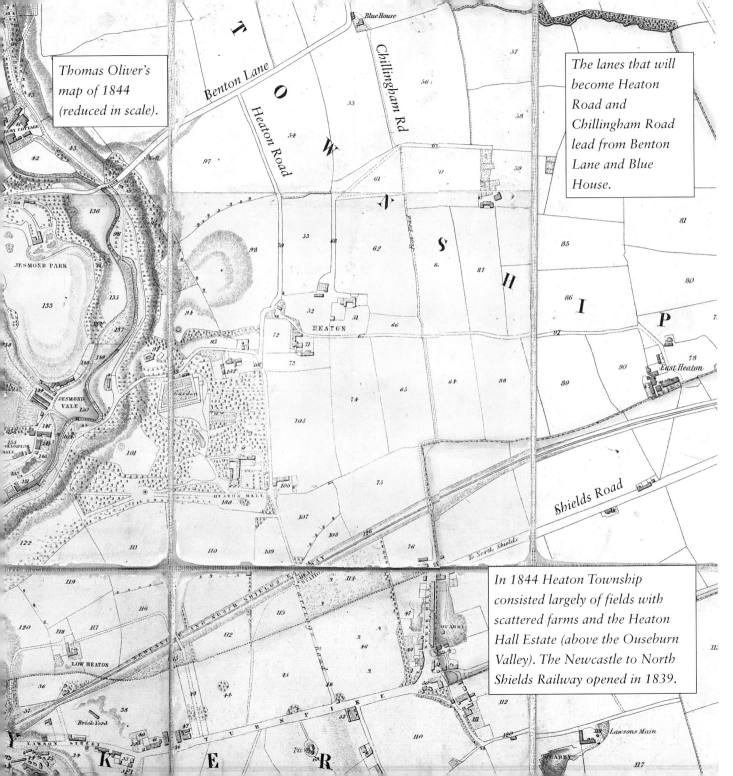

Thomas Oliver's map of 1844 (reduced in scale).

The lanes that will become Heaton Road and Chillingham Road lead from Benton Lane and Blue House.

In 1844 Heaton Township consisted largely of fields with scattered farms and the Heaton Hall Estate (above the Ouseburn Valley). The Newcastle to North Shields Railway opened in 1839.

Hactone, Hoton, Heaton ... the township high above the Ouseburn

Nearly two miles to the east of central Newcastle lies the popular suburb of Heaton. It covers nearly one square mile. Most of Heaton is now tightly packed with housing, shops and other amenities but there are also three spacious public parks covering about 70 acres or 12 per cent of the suburb.

Heaton has (and had) some historical buildings that illustrate its eventful and interesting past.

Hadrian's Wall, when built nearly 2000 years ago, ran parallel and very close to the south side of today's Shields Road. No doubt the availability of so much stone, almost begging to be recycled, determined the line of the turnpike (or toll road, known in more recent times as Shields Road) from Newcastle to Tynemouth, as it appears on early 18th century maps.

Newcastle's boundaries were widened in 1835 to include not only Heaton but also Byker, Elswick, Jesmond and Westgate. For the purpose of this book, High Heaton has been excluded and Heaton's boundaries are defined as Stephenson Road / Coast Road to the north, the main railway line to Scotland to the east, Shields Road (north side only) to the south and the Ouseburn valley to the west.

Until the 1870s, most of Heaton remained agricultural with only a handful of farms interspersed with scattered coal pits. The relatively small number of residents at that time would probably have depended on these two sources of work. The population of Heaton in 1841 was 220, by 1871 it was 257, but by 1901 it had risen dramatically to 22,913.

Change began with the arrival of the railway. In 1839 the new Newcastle to North Shields railway sliced through the southern part of Heaton and provided a passenger station near Heaton Road as well

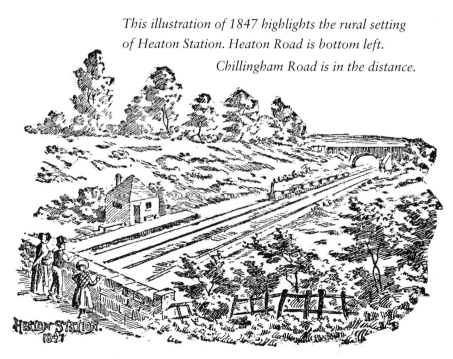

This illustration of 1847 highlights the rural setting of Heaton Station. Heaton Road is bottom left. Chillingham Road is in the distance.

HEATON STATION. 1847

as a toll footpath alongside the track of the rail viaduct across the Ouseburn valley. Less than a decade later the main east coast railway was in use. There was a large marshalling yard at Heaton Junction that created a lot of employment. In 1879 the Riverside line (now defunct) opened, primarily to serve the growing number of industrial businesses springing up on the banks of the river Tyne. From this point, Heaton rapidly expanded into a popular residential area.

Housing development in Heaton spread initially from its south west corner near the top of Byker Bank to include the area of farmland between Shields Road and the existing railway. The opening of Byker Road Bridge in 1878 greatly accelerated the building of further dwellings, which then spread northwards on either side of what is now Heaton Road. Later, there was a similar development on both sides of what is today Chillingham Road, most of which had been a mere 'foot road', flanked by fields, from Byker to Benton.

By 1901, most of Heaton to the south of Simonside Terrace (where there was a tram terminus for a number of years) was packed with dwellings, leaving the remaining area to the north as farmland. The bulk of this was used for housing development and completed before the outbreak of the First World War. However, there were still some parts, particularly near to the northern boundary and in the vicinity of Heaton Hall (demolished in 1933), that were not developed until the 1930s or later.

Looking north from near the junction of Shields Road and Heaton Road, around 1905.

Heaton History

Heaton is first recorded in a legal document of 1157 as HACTONA and then in 1279 as HOTON. Both names almost certainly refer to a village or settlement above the banks of the Ouseburn. Heaton was part of the barony of Ellingham, owned in the 12th century by William de Grenville, so its early history is similar to that of the neighbouring township of Jesmond. Sometime before 1267 Adam of Jesmond, a descendant of Grenville and one-time Sheriff of Northumberland, built himself a tower house for security at Heaton. Some remains of this building are still visible in Heaton Park.

KING JOHN'S CHAPEL, HEATON PARK.

In 1299 King Edward I visited the tower house, many years after the death of his old supporter Adam of Jesmond. On this visit a boy-bishop recited the vespers of St Nicholas before the king in his chapel (assumed to be part of or near to the tower house) at Heaton and the king donated 40s (£2) to be divided among the choir boys. In 1617 King James I visited Newcastle on his way to Scotland and stayed at Heaton Hall with the owner Henry Babington, who was rewarded with a knighthood because of the superb entertainment he provided.

The township of Heaton then passed through various families until in 1692 the Mitfords of Seghill sold their half share to Nicholas Ridley of Newcastle. Ridley's son Richard was to build a new Heaton Hall in 1713, probably on the site of an earlier building. Later the other half of Heaton was sold to Matthew White, another Newcastle merchant, who bequeathed it to his sister Elizabeth and her husband (and cousin) Matthew Ridley in his will dated 1755. Their eldest son Matthew became the first in a series of descendants all with the name of Sir Matthew White Ridley.

The whole of Heaton remained in the possession of the White Ridleys of Blagdon until 1841, when a succeeding Sir Matthew White Ridley sold Heaton Hall and grounds to Addison Langhorn Potter, a local industrialist. In the same year Sir Matthew sold the northern part of the township to Armorer Donkin, a well-known local solicitor, who bequeathed it in 1851 to Sir William G. Armstrong. The remainder of the township was purchased by Lord Armstrong from the White Ridleys in 1868. Ten years later the Potters sold their 22.5 acre grounds (their back garden) to Newcastle Corporation. It was opened to the public in 1879 as Heaton Park. In 1880 the western part of Heaton, 28.5 acres on the banks of the Ouseburn, was officially opened as Armstrong Park, having been donated by Lord Armstrong to Newcastle Corporation as a public park two years previously. In the 1930s Heaton Hall was replaced by housing.

The Armstrong connection has resulted in many of the streets in the north of the suburb having place names (such as Rothbury Terrace, or Simonside Terrace) associated with Armstrong's Cragside estate.

Above, the Armstrong Guns on the Pavilion terrace. Right, Heaton Park Lake, with the bear cage far left (see page 65).

THE TERRACE, HEATON PARK, NEWCASTLE ON TYNE.

Heaton Park, The Lake, Newcastle

Heaton farms

The earliest known map of Heaton to mark farms and fields is dated 1844 (see page 6) and identifies five farms, which, together with their surrounding agricultural land, effectively cover most of the suburb. This land lay between two important thoroughfares that existed at the time. One of these routes was the Newcastle to North Shields turnpike at the southern boundary, while at the northern border, Benton Lane carried traffic between Newcastle and Benton. Elsewhere in the area there were only minor foot roads and lanes, which generally gave access to farms, collieries or places of habitation. Some of these routes developed into modern roads such as the Carriage Drive that led from Heaton Hall to the North Shields turnpike, which became the earliest part of Heaton Road.

More or less at the centre of Heaton, near the junction of Heaton Road and Simonside Terrace, was Heaton Farm, which at nearly 155 acres was the largest of the five farms in terms of acreage. The 1841 census recorded 57 people living in 13

Above, farm buildings joined on to the House of Adam (King John's Palace) around 1860, below, Heaton Park around 1900.

HEATON PARK, NEWCASTLE.

dwellings including a grocer's shop. The 35-year-old unmarried farmer's household included three servants plus a lodger, and his 17 fields covered the area to the east of what is now Heaton Road and reached as far north as Benton Lane.

East Heaton Farm, in the south east corner of the suburb, was the next largest farm at about 130 acres. In 1841 there were 68 people living in 14 homes, including the farmer who looked after 12 fields lying mainly north of the railway and extending westwards to abut the fields of Heaton Farm. Later, railway infrastructure replaced farm buildings.

The Heaton Hall Estate had its own farm, which stood close to the junction of Heaton Road and Roxburgh Place. Several fields, some of which straddled the railway, belonged to the farm as well as a market garden making up a total area of nearly 90 acres, excluding the grounds of Heaton Hall. According to the 1841 census there were five people living in two farm buildings.

A fourth farm lay in the south west part of the suburb, near to the junction of Stratford Road and Bolingbroke Street. Known as Low Heaton, in 1841 the farm consisted of five people living in two buildings, one of which housed a 28-year-old farmer, his wife and a servant. A 70-year-old couple lived in the other dwelling.

The last, and by far the smallest, farm was at Byker Hill, close to the junction today of Shields Road and the south end of Chillingham Road. There were only two fields, one on either side of the railway. In 1841 13 people lived there in two separate dwellings. The farmer, his wife and three children

The Temple, Heaton Park, Newcastle.

occupied one building, while a publican and his family, including three boys all teenage colliers, lived in the second building. It is said that in 1790 John Wesley preached to the community at Byker Hill.

Heaton's coalmines

It is not known for certain when mining began in Heaton. 'Accessible coal' is mentioned in a legal document of 1482, which refers to working with simple tools in shallow pits near an outcrop of coal. A small-scale map, dated c.1600, marks three pits in Heaton but does not name them or give their exact location.

In 1678, Robert Mitford, a Newcastle merchant and part owner of Heaton, obtained a lease from Newcastle Corporation for 'three keelrooms (berths) lying on the east side of the Ouseburn,' which perhaps indicated a colliery of reasonable size nearby. The colliery's position remains unknown but was probably between what is now Stratford Grove and South View West beside the banks of the Ouseburn. It would have been near the tidal limit of the Ouseburn and close to the existing waggonway leading from Jesmond down the Ouseburn valley. Drainage problems appear to have caused the colliery to be abandoned in 1689.

The next known colliery in Heaton began in around 1727 when the Grand Allies, a monopolist partnership of regional coal owners, obtained a lease from the Ridley family to mine coal. The Grand Allies were probably encouraged to invest £40,000 in developing what became known as Heaton Banks Colliery because of the recent availability of Thomas Newcomen's new atmospheric steam engine for the drainage of mines. This colliery comprised 18 separate pits, spaced about 300 yards apart, in the area now covered by Heaton and Armstrong Parks as well as Jesmond Dene. The large number of pit shafts in use at this time was necessary because of ventilation problems in mines. They were partly solved by having a coal fire burning at the foot of one shaft, enabling foul air to rise and escape up that shaft and be replaced by fresh air drawn down a second connected shaft. Heaton Banks Colliery became one of the 'great collieries of the period' with a waggonway to the river Tyne at St Anthony's. However, as with the earlier Mitford Colliery, serious flooding was to result in its demise in 1745, at which point production was moved to Longbenton.

The invention of the more efficient steam engine by James Watt in 1769 almost certainly prompted the opening of further pits in Heaton. In 1792 permission was obtained to sink three pits to be collectively known as Heaton Main Colliery and to open any necessary waggonways. 'Main' in a colliery name implied that this was the most important seam of coal to be worked. Only a small area of land (maximum 4 acres) was allowed at each pit for the pithead, workshops and dwellings, which is probably why no colliery villages developed. Most workers lived elsewhere.

The first of these three pits opened in 1796 at the south east corner of the suburb near East Heaton Farm, an area later covered by the railway sidings of Heaton Junction. It became known as the Engine Pit, was 516ft deep and with the aid of Watt's steam engine it could raise and lower coal, miners, ponies and water. The mine closed in 1821.

Between 1801 and 1803 two more pits were opened. The Middle Pit began in the area now surrounded by Addycombe Terrace, Cartington Terrace, Whitefield Terrace and Biddlestone Road and continued until 1852 when flooding became an issue.

The second pit to open was the Far Pit, in what is now High Heaton, where in 1815 a total of 75 men and boys lost their lives. These miners were trapped about 330ft below ground by a sudden inrush of water from the adjacent and former workings of the Heaton Banks Colliery approximately beneath the junction of Heaton Road and Meldon Terrace, nearly one mile from the pit head. It took several months to recover the bodies (and 37 horses) most of whom it is thought died of suffocation because there remained nearby lumps of uneaten horse flesh, an adequate supply of spring water and 'two pounds of unburned candles'. These victims of the mining disaster are remembered by 75 trees planted at the Spinney, a small landscaped area near the site of the former Far Pit. This pit closed in 1827 and was superseded by Benton Colliery alongside the Coxlodge waggonway, near to its crossing with Benton Road about half a mile to the north east.

Another waggonway connected all the pits of the Heaton Main Colliery to the river Tyne staithes, a distance of just over three miles. Early steam locomotives (known as 'travelling engines') would have been a common sight moving between the pastures and fields of rural Heaton.

Finally, during the 1850s and probably the 1860s, there was another smaller colliery near the junction of Heaton Park Road and the railway. It was associated with a nearby fireclay mine, quarry and brickworks. Heaton Park Road School replaced the colliery in 1879 and today multi-storey flats (Heaton Park Court) occupy the site.

This early travelling engine, the Steam Elephant, was in use at Wallsend Colliery from 1815, but similar ones operated at Heaton.

This view of the Ouseburn Valley, looking north from Low Heaton, was painted by J. Brown in 1860. The foreground area is today covered by landfill and the City Stadium. The Ouseburn is diverted in a culvert.

In the lower foreground is Low Heaton Haugh in front of Ouseburn Road. This house and its gardens belonged to Henry Turner, a colliery owner and tile manufacturer. To the right are the Ouseburn Cement Works, later to become the Ouseburn Soap Works. Above the quarry face is a chimney which may have belonged to the Cement Works. There were also clay pits there belonging to the brick and tile works. This part of Heaton is now covered by Newington Road, Hotspur Street etc.

In the distance to the left we can see Jesmond Vale. A footbridge over the burn leads to rural Sandyford.

Reduced from the 1899 revision of OS. Heaton is about 20 years into its development.

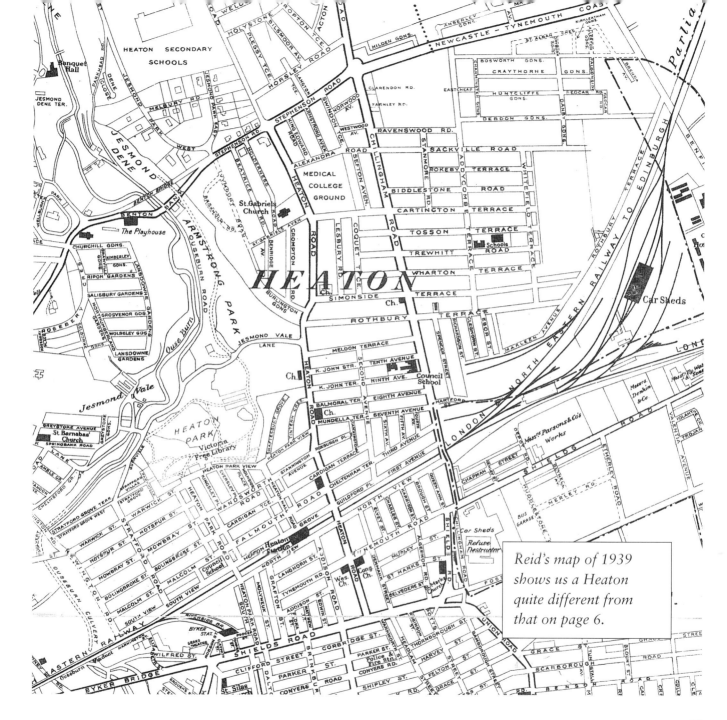

Reid's map of 1939 shows us a Heaton quite different from that on page 6.

Exploring Heaton

The following pages are set out in the form of four walks through Heaton, but if you prefer, just take an armchair trip around the sights of this interesting suburb.

We have used Reid's map of Heaton in 1939 (opposite, slightly enlarged from the original) to guide you through each walk, along with the OS revision of 1899 (below) of the same area as a comparison. Compare these maps with Thomas Oliver's survey of 1844 pictured on page 6 and you will see how Heaton changed from a rural settlement of farms and isolated houses to a bustling and crowded residential and industrial part of Newcastle in less than 100 years.

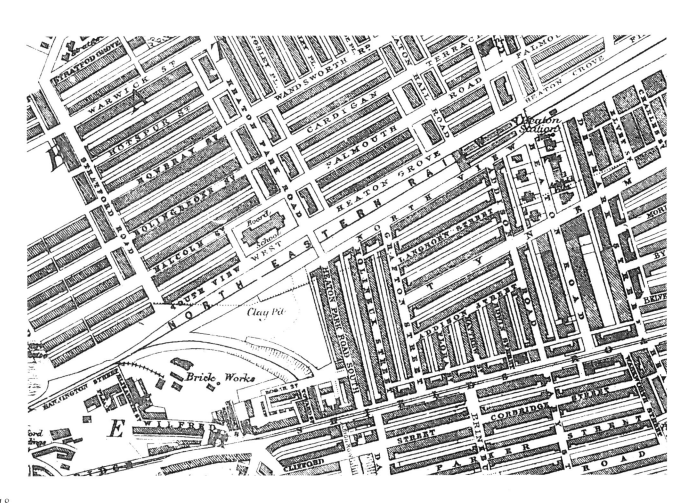

Walk 1: From Lloyds Bank, Shields Road, circular

1. Lloyd's Bank Ltd.

2. Trustee Savings Bank

3. Leighton Primitive Methodist Chapel

4. Bainbridge Memorial Chapel and Congregational Church

5. Addison Hotel, Addison Road

6. Heaton Electric Palace, Heaton Road

7. Heaton Station

8. Heaton Park Road School

9. Heaton Park Road North

10. Stratford Road

11. Viaduct Hotel, Wilfred Street

12. Grand Theatre, Wilfred Street

13. Ford Arms, Wilfred Street

14. Apollo Cinema, Shields Road

15. Beavan's Corner

16. Shields Road

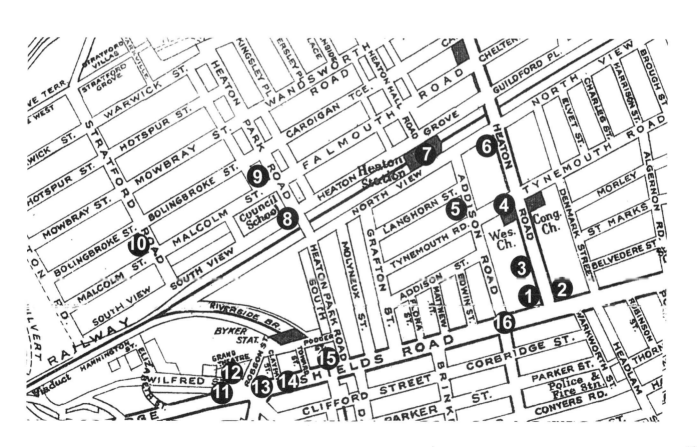

1. Lloyd's Bank Ltd., Shields Road

The attractive three storey stone building on the left, with classical architectural features, stands at the corner of Shields Road and Heaton Road. It opened in around 1908 as Lloyds Bank Ltd. and replaced two 30-year-old shops. Look out for 'LLOYDS BANK LIMITED' inscribed on a rainwater hopper.

Several years ago Lloyds TSB moved across Heaton Road into the former Trustee Savings Bank building, just visible on the right. Their original building remains unoccupied.

The photograph, dated around 1910, looks along Heaton Road from its junction with Shields Road.

2. Trustee Savings Bank, Shields Road

The main entrance to the bank was from Shields Road, to the right of the illustration below, with a second door in Heaton Road to the left. Managers occupied the first floor and above them lived the caretaker. They shared an entrance into Heaton Road. The original plans for the building included a clock tower for the benefit of local people who didn't own watches. This must have been too expensive and instead an attractive clock was placed high up at the corner of the new building.

Trustee Savings Banks were set up by Act of Parliament in 1817, for 'the safe custody and increase of the small savings of the industrious classes'. At the opening ceremony in 1904 it was said that 'a man who had a deposit in a savings bank could never be hard up'. Also 'there was only one way to save money effectually and that was to put something on one side out of the weekly earnings, and insist on making the rest suffice' Lloyds TSB now occupy the building.

3. Leighton Primitive Methodist Chapel

The buildings on this part of Heaton Road, near its junction with Shields Road, were photographed in around 1910. They are almost unrecognisable today. Not only have both chapels disappeared but the neat row of substantial terraced houses in between, with their enclosed front gardens, have been converted into commercial premises with little regard for appearance.

Leighton Primitive Methodist Chapel, on the left, opened in 1877 and was one of the earliest buildings on Heaton Road. Designed in the Italianate style with a broad pedimented front, the chapel moved here from the Ouseburn Valley where it had been known as the Ballast Hills Chapel, with William Brogg Leighton as its principal lay preacher. Although a master printer by trade, he was also heavily involved in assisting the underprivileged members of society, so the site of the Ballast Hills Chapel was renamed Leighton Street. The new building in Heaton Road was also named in his memory.

Nearly 90 years later, the Leighton Chapel merged with the Wesleyan Methodists at the Bainbridge Memorial Chapel, a short distance along Heaton Road. It is identified on this photograph by its tall tower. The Leighton Chapel was replaced by a mini supermarket (recently closed).

The row of houses between the chapels was built in the late 1870s and its occupants at the date of this photograph included a few surgeons, a master mariner, a furniture dealer, a joiner, a dentist and a couple of clerks.

4. Cuthbert Bainbridge Memorial Methodist Chapel and Heaton Congregational Church

Here is another view looking north along Heaton Road in around 1905 with two non-conformist buildings opposite each other at the junction with Tynemouth Road. The Cuthbert Bainbridge Memorial Methodist Chapel on the left opened in 1885. The site was donated by Emerson Muschamp Bainbridge, founder of the Newcastle

department store. Cuthbert Bainbridge, his eldest son, had died of typhus aged 32. He had been a class leader in the Wesleyan movement with a deep interest in the Band of Hope.

Designed by J. Oswald & Son, the chapel had a lofty tower with a pyramid roof. It housed school rooms, office space and recreation rooms. In the recreation rooms poor women were taught to make clothes for themselves, using material provided cheaply by Bainbridge's.

Following the merger with the Presbyterians further along Heaton Road, the chapel buildings were demolished and replaced by a Youth and Community Centre (known as The Ark) and apartments.

Facing across Heaton Road is the much smaller and very plain Congregational Church, completed in 1882 and designed by Oliver and Leeson. This church became an Elim Pentecostal Church in 1915 and continues to function as such.

By the late 1880s Heaton Road was largely built up as far as the railway bridge. Beyond that lay fields.

5. The Addison Hotel

Originally built in the mid 1870s along with surrounding residential property, the Addison Hotel stood at the corner of Addison Road and Tynemouth Road. The name Addison originates from Addison Langhorn Potter, the owner of nearby Heaton Hall at that time.

Rebuilt in 1890, it was extended six years later by local architects Septimus Oswald and Son to become the largest

Geoff Philips

pub in the area. It was also one of the most important in the East End with a full-time staff of eight. It may have been popular because it was near the footbridge over the railway at Heaton Station that gave access from 'dry' Heaton, north of the line.

Inside the pub, there was a magnificent arcade of elaborate wooden tracery between the grill room and the buffet that reflected the high level of local craft skills in the late Victorian period.

The Addison is pictured here in 1966. It closed three years later and the whole area was redeveloped with low rise terraced housing connected by intricate pathways and open squares with a minimum of access roads. Most of the original street names have been retained but are now followed by 'close' or 'walk' rather than 'street' or 'road'.

6. Heaton Electric Palace

Built on the site of the former Newcastle and Gateshead Gas Company's workshops (built around 1905), the Heaton Electric Palace opened in 1910. Many cinemas, opened in Newcastle around this time. Known as 'The favourite resort of Heatonians' and considered 'homely and select', it also presented variety shows, had a billiard hall and roller skating rink (later converted into a ballroom). It stood at the corner of Heaton Road and North View. The pit had 223 leather tip-up seats at 2d, there were 390 plush tip-ups in the stalls at 4d and in the circle 312 plush tip-ups cost 6d. A full house in 1910, including private boxes, raised about £18. The cinema closed in 1961 and is now a bingo hall.

The top view, taken around 1912, looks along Heaton Road towards Shields Road with a pedestrian entrance to Heaton railway station (now removed) on the bridge and in front of the Electric Palace. In the distance is the tower of the Cuthbert Bainbridge Memorial Methodist Chapel.

The lower view, from around 1949 is taken from the opposite direction looking towards the Electric Palace with the Heaton Road railway bridge in the background, largely obscured by traffic. Just visible above the nearer vehicle is the upper part of a Finlay's kiosk. These kiosks sold tobacco, confectionary and newspapers and were usually found near railway stations.

7. Heaton Station, 1978

For nearly 50 years the first Heaton Station consisted only of a small wooden booking office with a couple of open platforms on either side of the rail track. There was no shelter for waiting passengers. The track and

station were in a deep cutting almost a mile long and conveniently out of sight for the residents of Heaton Hall, which stood a few hundred yards away to the north across open fields. Built for the Newcastle and North Shields Railway which opened in 1839, the station's importance grew following the 1847 opening of the route between Newcastle and Tweedmouth, which would become part of the main East Coast line (see the drawing on page 7 for a very early view). Trains at this time travelled on the right hand side of the track! By 1900, this area had been fully urbanised.

In 1887, when the rail tracks were doubled, Heaton Station was moved a few hundred yards to the other side of Heaton Road at the junction of Heaton Grove and Heaton Hall Road. Shortage of space resulted in a new and largely wooden station straddling the widened rail tracks. This unusual station contained offices, waiting rooms, and at least two kiosks, as well as providing a public walking route connecting with North View. Ramps led down from the structure to the platforms alongside the track. Contemporary sources reveal that this unique building 'always smelt of a strange amalgam, possibly including Jeyes Fluid, kippers and carbolic'.

The photograph above features the passenger express train hauled by British Rail locomotive No. 60012 'Commonwealth of Australia' as it passed beneath the station structure in the 1950s.

The picture on the left, looking in the opposite direction, was taken two years before the station closed in 1980. It was subsequently demolished.

8. Heaton Park Road School

Heaton Park Road School opened in 1879, on the site of a former small colliery, to meet the rapidly rising population in the area and was the fourth Board School to be opened in Newcastle. Designed to cater for 1,064 pupils by the architects Austin Johnson & Hicks, it cost £11,579 and replaced temporary accommodation in local buildings.

Stone built with a red tile roof and mullioned and transomed windows, this two-storey school also had an attached four-roomed cottage for a caretaker. Infants were on the ground floor with other scholars on the floor above and 'the lavatories and hat room' on a mezzanine level. The largest classroom, apart from the assembly halls, was designed to contain 100 children. A classroom for girls was fully equipped with appliances and a kitchen range to teach cookery. Separate covered playgrounds were provided for boys and girls.

A striking feature of the school's appearance was the 100ft ventilation tower. All rooms were heated by hot water fed from a furnace in the basement and then air was extracted by shafts connected to the tower.

The school was demolished in the late 1950s (as pictured) and replaced in 1960 by Heaton Park Court, the City's first ever skyscraper block of flats. Designed by the City architect George Kenyon, it became the first tower-type block in the country to have six flats, rather than the customary four, on each floor. The building is twelve storeys high and contains 72 one- and two-bedroom flats.

These children were photographed at Heaton Park Road School around 1885.

In 1870 the Education Act established school boards to build and manage non-denominational elementary schools paid for out of the local rates. Boards were empowered to make school compulsory between five and 13, but were not absolutely required to. There were many exceptions. In 1880 a further Act (the Mundella Act) came into force which made it compulsory for all children aged between five and 10 to attend school (though by the 1890s only around 82% of children attended). There were also penalties for the illegal employment of children aged 10 - 13. Many poor children truanted as families needed the money they could earn. In addition, fees might be payable until a change in the law in 1891 made education free. By 1893 children had to attend school until they were 11 and in 1899 this was extended to age 12. Several schools were built in Heaton as the population increased.

9. Heaton Park Road North

A view of Heaton Park Road North in 1910 looking towards Heaton Park, at the far end, from the corner of Malcolm Street (left) and Falmouth Road (right). This mixture of houses and shops, largely built in the 1880s, has hardly changed except that the types of shops have altered dramatically. Instead of the traditional fishmonger, butcher, confectioner, fruiterer, draper and hardware dealer, there is now a mini supermarket, an off-licence, a ladies' hair stylist, a barber, a sandwich shop and a few premises dealing in second hand goods.

This area is now popular with university students and the road is a very busy commuter route with frequent bus services.

Heaton Park Road South, between the railway and Shields Road was originally known as Cook Street (named after a local councillor) and dates from the 1870s.

10. Stratford Road

A view of Stratford Road in around 1910, from near the corner of Malcolm Street towards the next junction at Bolingbroke Street and then beyond as the road eventually dips down into the Ouseburn Valley.

The premises on the right, dating from the mid 1880s were mainly shops, most of which have now been converted for residential use.

Similarly the shops on the left, constructed about five years later, have all been refitted as student accommodation.

At the time of this photograph the shops included grocers, butchers and confectioners.

Interestingly, a gable end at the rear of Stratford Road and adjacent to South View West has a large head and shoulder portrait of William Shakespeare painted on the brick wall – a probable connection with the historically named streets in the vicinity (Hotspur, Bolingbroke, Mowbray, Warwick and Malcolm).

11. The Viaduct Hotel, Wilfred Street, 1961

The Viaduct Hotel originated as a private house, dating from at least 1840, in the middle of a terrace of similar houses in Lawson Street. Named after a well-known local 16th century land-owning family, Lawson Street connected Ouseburn Road in the Ouseburn Valley (before infill in the early 20th century) with Byker Toll Bar on the main road between Newcastle and North Shields. In around 1873 Lawson Street was renamed Wilfred Street.

By 1844 the house had become a beer house. The Beer Act of 1830 permitted any ratepayer to sell beer on his own premises without a magistrate's license, in an attempt to counter the easy access to spirits at that time. This Act was repealed in 1869.

Around 1850 the premises became known as the Ouseburn Viaduct Inn, named after the nearby railway viaduct which had opened in 1839. It was re-named The Viaduct Hotel in about 1890. This hotel stood opposite the Grand Theatre and was well patronized by theatre-goers, staff and artistes, including Kenneth More the celebrated actor. For a while in the 1890s the secretary of Newcastle United Football Club had his office in the building.

Most of the houses in Wilfred Street were demolished in the 1960s. The hotel closed in 1977 and the building is now used as The Byker Bridge Workshop.

12. The Grand Theatre, 1910

A suburban theatre for Newcastle was a novel experiment when the Grand Theatre opened in 1896 with a production of *The Taming of the Shrew*. Other Shakespearian plays were performed during the remainder of that first week.

Designed to seat 2,500, this impressive building stood in Wilfred Street close to the eastern end of Byker Bridge. The theatre abutted onto three streets, so the architect, William Hope, provided six separate entrances and exits so that different classes of theatregoer would not have to meet. The main entrance, surmounted by an imposing corner turret, was reserved for patrons of the circle and private boxes while the others gave access to the cheaper seats in the pit stalls and gallery. A large, elegant marble staircase led from the main entrance to the most expensive part of the theatre, which had 'tip-up chairs upholstered in terra-cotta plush'. In an attempt to create an atmosphere of cheerfulness, in contrast to the drab world outside the theatre, the auditorium was liberally decorated with gilt.

For much of the Grand's 58-year existence as a place of entertainment it alternated between theatre and cinema. It began and ended as a theatre but silent films featured from about 1910, followed 20 years later by the ever popular 'talkies'.

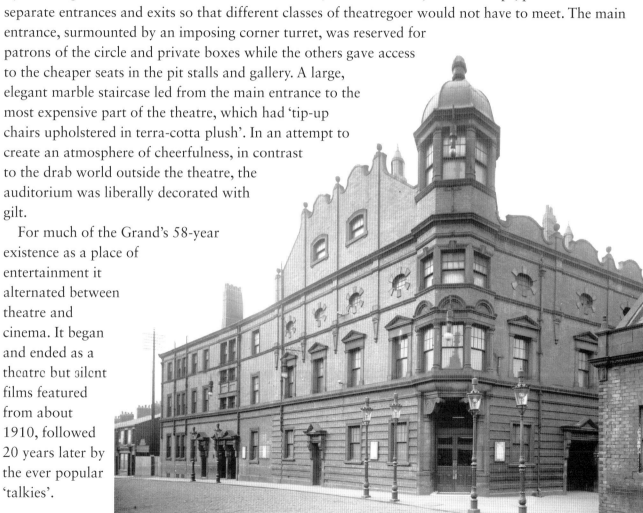

Many of the theatrical productions at the Grand, which included modern dramas and musical comedies, followed successful London performances. During the late 1930s Kenneth More, the well known actor, often appeared in repertory at the Grand and was known to enjoy a tipple at the nearby Viaduct public house. For many years Wilfred Street had the distinction of having three pubs (including the Viaduct) within less than 200 yards.

The Grand closed in 1954 and spent the next ten years as a warehouse for a firm of builders' merchants. After a fire in 1964 the building was demolished. A purpose-built furniture recycling warehouse now occupies the site.

The Chinese Bungalow featured at The Grand in June 1931.

Grand Theatre,

BYKER BRIDGE, NEWCASTLE.

Lessees—WELDON WATTS & Co. Managing Director—WELDON WATTS.

UNDOUBTEDLY ONE OF THE MOST MAGNIFICENT
THEATRES IN THE COUNTY.

WILL OPEN MONDAY, JULY 27,

With the famous Shakespearian Actor, F. R. BENSON, supported by Mrs F. R. BENSON, and his Famous Company.

MONDAY, JULY 27th, TAMING OF THE SHREW.
Petruchio....Mr F. R. Benson. Catherine....Mrs F. R. Benson.

TUESDAY, JULY 28th, MERCHANT OF VENICE.
Shylock......Mr F. R. Benson. Portia........Mrs F. R. Benson.

WEDNESDAY, JULY 29th, TAMING OF THE SHREW.

THURSDAY, JULY 30th, HAMLET.
Hamlet......Mr F. R. Benson. Ophelia.......Mrs F. R. Benson.

FRIDAY, JULY 31st, AS YOU LIKE IT.
Orlando ...Mr F. R. Benson. Rosalind......Mrs F. R. Benson.

SATURDAY, AUGUST 1st, RICHARD III.
Richard......Mr F R. Benson. Elizabeth ....Mrs F. R. Benson.

POPULAR PRICES :—Private Boxes, £1 11s 6d and £1 1s ; Dress Circle, 2s 6d ; Second Circle and Orchestra Stalls (Tip-up-Chairs), 1s 6d, if booked, 2s ; Pit Stalls, 1s ; Pit and Amphitheatre, 6d ; Gallery, 4d.
Doors open at 7, commence 7·30. Box Office open 11 till 3. National Telephone, 6,544.

MONDAY, Aug. 3rd, Mr G. W. Daventry's Company in
THE INDIAN MUTINY.

The advert left appeared in Northern Gossip in July 1896.

13. The Ford Arms, Wilfred Street, 1967

Before 1928, when it was rebuilt, the Ford Arms occupied a converted house on the same site on Lawson Street (later renamed Wilfred Street). The house dated back to at least 1840 and was occupied at that time by a tailor. During the mid 1860s the premises (like the Viaduct Hotel) became a beer house (the beer retailer was also a butcher) and then in the late 1870s the building obtained a magistrate's licence and was renamed the Ford Arms.

It is thought the pub was named in memory of Mary Ford whose generous dowry in 1857 helped her husband, Christopher Thompson Maling to expand his existing pottery business in the nearby Lower Ouseburn into two purpose-built factories known as Ford 'A' and Ford 'B'. At one time they employed around 1,000 people. A new thoroughfare alongside the Ford A pottery was named Ford Street in 1859.

In later years the pub was re-named 'Wor Jackie's' after Jackie Milburn, who played for Newcastle United between 1943 and 1957 and was famous for his prolific goal scoring ability.

A vehicle service station now occupies the site of the former pub.

14 The Apollo Cinema, 1967

The Apollo Cinema stood in Shields Road opposite the top of Byker Bank and not far from the Grand Theatre in Wilfred Street. Designed by local architect Pascal Stienlet, it opened in 1933 with seats for 1,650. The outside was cement rendered in white, while inside was tastefully decorated in orange, cream and blue with some geometric patterns on the walls and ceiling. The carpets and seating were blue. Initially there were two evening performances each day, with prices ranging from 6d in the stalls to 9d and 1s in the circle. At this time a staff of 30, excluding management, ran the cinema, which was regarded in the trade as the 'Apollo Goldmine' with consistently packed houses. Two unusual features were large comfortable heated waiting rooms and a free car park, reckoned to be the first of its kind in Newcastle. An 18 table billiard hall was added in 1935.

This successful enterprise came to an abrupt end in 1941 when a German bomb demolished the building over night (fortunately there were no casualties) and it was 15 years before the cinema re-opened. The billiard hall escaped damage. In an attempt to halt declining attendances, bingo replaced films for a couple of years in the 1960s. Multi screens were introduced in the next decade.

The Apollo finally closed in 1983. Today, a large purpose-built supermarket more than covers the site.

15. Beavan's Corner, Shields Road, Heaton Park Road, around 1910

Beavan's Great Summer Sale appears to be successfully underway in this sunlit view of Shields Road. This corner shop, at the junction of Shields Road and Heaton Park Road, was the original site of Frederick Beavan's first drapery business, which opened in 1875. Prudhoe-born Frederick, aged just 28, walked the 12 miles from Prudhoe each way every day, paying a penny to use the footway over the Ouseburn railway viaduct. Byker Bridge had not yet opened. Understandably it was not long before Beavan and his wife found living space above their shop until they were able to afford larger accommodation elsewhere in the locality.

By the turn of the century Beavan had acquired premises on both sides of Heaton Park Road as far as

No. 90   Shields Road, Byker.

the junction with Roger Street. Further expansion occurred around 1910, when a major rebuild took place on the opposite corner of Heaton Park Road, which included the existing imposing double-storey white stone building with attractive fan-shaped upper windows. (See the back cover of this book for a view of the rear of Beavan's in 1914.)

Following Beavan's death in 1928, more premises were acquired further down Shields Road and extra storeys were added to their existing buildings along Heaton Park Road. By this time the business was a department store that included a drapery, men's outfitters, house furnishings, upholstery, ironmongery and general items. Many of their products were made in their own workshops and retailed under the brand name of 'Beavona'.

In 1954 the business was sold to Great Universal Stores after the last of Beavan's four sons had died. About 60 years earlier both of Beavan's daughters had married into the Fenwick family, another of Newcastle's departmental store dynasties. Interestingly, Frederick Beavan's grandfather, a Dr Frederick Beavan, had served as a surgeon on board Nelson's HMS *Victory*.

The photograph right, taken in 1996, looks along Heaton Park Road from its junction with Shields Road. The tall brick building has now been converted into apartments while most of the other buildings on Shields Road function as retail units. It is still possible to see the name 'F Beavan Ltd. Ironmongers and Furnishers' above one of the Shields Road premises.

Malcolm Maybury

16. Shields Road, early 1950s, looking west

A policeman (in a white coat) can be seen in front of the trolley bus controlling traffic at the then busy junction of Shields Road, Raby Street and Addison Road. Trolley buses had been introduced to replace trams from the mid to late 1930s and were to operate in this area for about 30 years, being withdrawn between 1963 and 1966.

The tall, substantial building in the centre of the photograph functioned as the Masonic Hall Assembly Rooms from about 1903 and as the Masonic Billiard Hall until the 1950s. At the date of this photograph a printing works occupied the Billiard Hall, which was later taken over by an electrical contractor. A modern low-level double-storey building has now replaced the earlier structure. There is a betting shop on the corner site once occupied by the Masonic Hall.

Walk 2 from King John Palace (circular)

1. King John's Palace, Heaton Park
2. Refreshment Rooms, Armstrong Park
3. Sunken Path, Armstrong Park
4. King John's Well, Armstrong Park
5. Windmill and Bandstand, Armstrong Park
6. Heaton Road and Meldon Terrace
7. Heaton Road shops
8. St Theresa's Church
9. King John Street
10. Heaton Road shops
11. Balmoral Terrace
12. Heaton Baptist Church

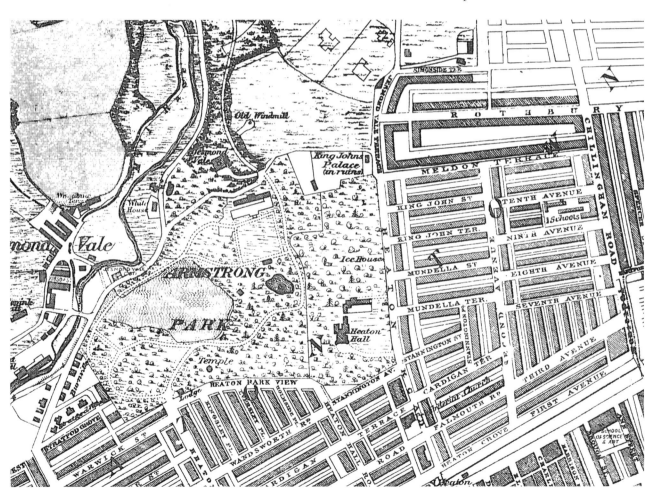

13. Mundella Terrace

14. Heaton Hall

15. Holmside Place and Kingsley Place

16. Armstrong Gun, Heaton Park

17. Temple, Heaton Park

18. Victoria Library, Heaton Park View

19. Garden Cottage, Heaton Park View

20. No. 190 Heaton Park Road

21. Burnville

22. The Lake, Heaton Park

23. Bowling Green and Pavilion, Heaton Park

24. Pavilion Terrace and Greens, Heaton Park

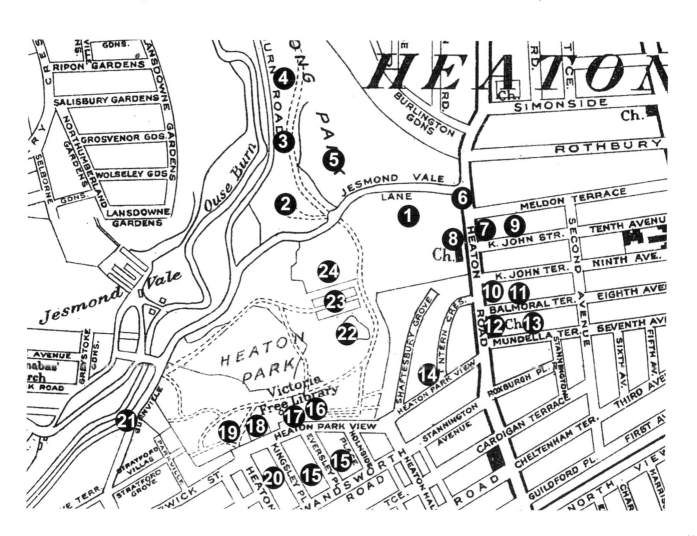

1. King John's Palace, Heaton Park, around 1890

These ruins in Heaton Park are thought to be the remains of the fortified tower house of Adam of Jesmond, a sheriff of Northumberland and keeper of the Royal Castle at Newcastle as well as the Lord of the Manor of Heaton and Jesmond. Such a stronghold was a necessity for all men of rank and wealth in the 13th century, when murder, arson and family feuds were commonplace. Adam was a staunch supporter of King Henry III and in return would probably have had little difficulty in obtaining royal permission to fortify his home with turrets, battlements, a moat and encircling wall.

Certainly in existence by 1267, confusingly the ruins are known locally as King John's Palace but apparently no part of Adam's tower house dates back to the reign of that monarch who died in 1216. A possible explanation is that an earlier Lord of the Manor of Heaton, Robert de Gaugy, may also have lived in this area. He had been a staunch supporter of King John (father of Henry III) in his struggle against the rebellious barons, so the King may well have lodged with Robert when visiting this area.

Adam's tower house had two storeys. The main room, used for communal eating and sleeping was on the upper floor and reached by climbing an external staircase to a door on the west side. At ground level the walls were six feet thick. Parts of the north and east walls (with window openings) rise to a height of 25 feet and traces of former doorways can be seen at first-floor level at the western side of the north wall.

Probably abandoned by the 17th century, the house with additions was later used as farm buildings until about 1840 (see the drawing on page 11).

2. Refreshment Rooms, Armstrong Park, 1931

This photograph shows a corner of the single-storey refreshment rooms in Armstrong Park, which opened in 1880. Formerly a dwelling, the building stood at the south end of the park, close to the Jesmond Vale Lane entrance. It was demolished during the 1960s and the site today is an open grassy area near trees well known as the 'Shoe Trees' (for obvious reasons).

The first known occupant of the house, in 1839, was Joseph Sewell, a 62-year-old earthenware manufacturer who had spent most of his working life running the St Anthony's Pottery. This rural retreat in Heaton may well have been his retirement home where he was to live for about another 20 years. For over 30 years Sewell had been managing the pottery in partnership with Armorer Donkin, a well known Newcastle solicitor who lived nearby at Jesmond Park. It was known as 'Sewell and Donkin' until Donkin's death in 1851. Interestingly the land in Heaton to which Sewell moved, was leased from Donkin. Perhaps the 58 acres of fields, some wooded plantations and the occasional cottage was intended to provide income during his retirement.

The pottery was very successful with a flourishing continental export trade and Tyneside's best lustre-ware. Sewell had other business interests besides his pottery, including a copperas (ferrous sulphate, used in the dyeing process and to make ink) works, also at St Anthony's, and was a managing partner in the St Lawrence glassworks owned by Sir Matthew White Ridley.

3. Sunken Path, Armstrong Park

Below the rustic bridge in Armstrong Park is a sunken stone-lined path about 250 yards long, which was created in around 1880 at an estimated cost of £421. Its purpose was to enable cattle grazing in fields at a higher level to reach alternative lower pasture near the Ouseburn without impeding, or being seen by, the public.

Although no longer in use, the path's distinctive stonework remains as does the bridge, which is now fitted with iron railings. Some of the quality stonework can be seen at the lower left of this illustration.

4. King John's Well, Armstrong Park

Although inscribed 'Ye Well of King John', this spring, like the so-called 'King John's Palace', has little or nothing to do with that particular monarch. The stone trough was found during excavations around Adam of Jesmond's tower house in the early 1880s and was moved here to collect water at one of the several springs on this hillside. Water continues to flow at this well but the metal drinking cups and their chains disappeared many years ago.

King John's Well, Newcastle-on-Tyne

Photo by F. Frith & Co., Reigate

On 16 August 1884, the Illustrated London News published a view (this is a detail) of Armstrong Park in their coverage of the visit of the Prince and Princess of Wales to Newcastle to open Jesmond Dene. The sunken path is clearly seen leading from the fields down to the Ouseburn. In the distance we can probably see the colliery houses of the High Heaton pit.

5. Heaton Windmill and Bandstand, Armstrong Park

A game of cricket is taking place in Armstrong Park in around 1910, with the remains of Heaton windmill in the central background and a Victorian bandstand a short distance to the right.

Built in the early 1700s, largely for the grinding of corn produced by local farmers, the tower mill originally had three floors surmounted by a timber structure with sails. Owned by Sir Matthew White Ridley for many years, it was (in 1827) one of 49 windmills in the vicinity of Newcastle, a surprisingly large number for an English town. The mill fell into disuse around 1840 following the introduction of steam-powered corn mills elsewhere in the region.

THE PLAYGROUND, HEATON PARK

The late Victorian bandstand is thought to have been dismantled in the late 1960s. It stood a short distance to the north east of the windmill at the foot of a gentle slope where temporary seating would have been arranged during summer months. Concerts were later moved to the Pavilion Terrace in Heaton Park. Nothing of the bandstand remains except for a section of the circular foundation now incorporated into a public path.

The young people, dressed in their best, in this view of the windmill from around 1910 look as if they are on an outing to the park.

6. Heaton Road

This image, from around 1915, shows three examples of wheeled transport by the junction of Heaton Road and Meldon Terrace. The No.10 tram is on its way back to the Royal Arcade via Jesmond Road and Northumberland Street, to complete a circular route that included City Road and Raby Street. To the left of the tram is a bungalow that once stood at the corner of Jesmond Vale Lane at the edge of the Heaton Hall Estate. The two-storey white brick residence to the right of the photograph is No. 1 Jesmond Vale Terrace, which at this time was occupied by a surgeon.

7. Heaton Road shops

How wonderful to be able to cycle with no other road user in sight! This was Heaton Road in about 1903. In the far distance can be seen the early stages of St Gabriel's Church.

This block of shops, relatively newly built, included a wine and spirit merchant, a baker, a fruiterer, a cycle manufacturer and a draper. Today there is a café, a hairdresser, a social club (a three shop space) and a restaurant. Opposite the shops are the grounds of the Heaton Hall Estate.

HEATON ROAD. 4456. G.H.N/C.

8. St Theresa's Roman Catholic Church, around 1971

This unusual church was consecrated and officially opened in 1971. It replaced a temporary building erected in 1927 in the grounds of the Heaton Hall Estate and with an entrance on Heaton Road. David Brown and Partners designed the octagonal church on a narrow strip of land with part of the building cantilevered on concrete piles on a hillside overlooking Heaton Park. Each of the eight sides forms a triangular gable with windows. Rising from the centre of the roof is a 70ft copper-clad steeple crowned with an orb and cross. The building is designed to seat 500 worshippers around three sides of the altar to give an uninterrupted view to everyone. Built of traditional materials, oak woodwork dominates inside and the ceiling is textured with sound-absorbing material.

Also on this site, known at one time as St Theresa's Park, is a Catholic School and a Presbytery.

9. King John Street

This view shows King John Street around 1910, looking from its junction with Heaton Road towards Chillingham Road at the far end. The crossing with Second Avenue can be seen in the middle distance with Tenth Avenue, linking it with Chillingham Road. The houses, now all with upper and lower bay windows, date from about 1895 and at the date of this photograph, their occupants had a wide range of occupations including an insurance agent, a blacksmith and a detective. The corner premises to the left of the photograph belonged to a wine and spirit merchant who remained on this site for about 30 years. The apparently mis-named King John's Palace is approximately behind the photographer on the other side of Heaton Road.

10. Heaton Road shops

This fine looking range of shops was the second retail centre to be built on Heaton Road in the late 1890s. The photograph was taken about a decade later. The shops were built in three blocks of seven, between Balmoral Terrace, immediately on the right and Meldon Terrace in the distance, with King John Terrace and King John Street in between. Heaton Hall Estate, which included the remains of the so-called King John's Palace, is on the left. In the far distance, the majestic tower of St Gabriel's Church is clearly visible.

At this time the shops focused on selling food and clothing. Today the mix is quite different and includes a restaurant, a men's social club, a tattoo studio, two firms dealing with student lettings and an Asian cuisine restaurant.

No. 93   Heaton Road, N C-on-Tyne.

11. Balmoral Terrace, around 1910

The photograph looks from Heaton Road along Balmoral Terrace towards the crossing with Second Avenue and beyond to Eighth Avenue.

The houses date from about 1895. Around 1910 the residents included a mixture of tradesmen, a travelling draper, a hay merchant and a compositor. A change in architecture can be seen as upstairs bay windows begin to appear about halfway along the terrace. All the railings and dormer windows have now been removed.

12. Heaton Baptist Church

After years of meetings held in private homes, rented rooms and, for a few years at the Denmark Street Hall, a site for a church was obtained in around 1895. It was on Heaton Road, virtually opposite Heaton Hall. The landowner, Charles John Potter, offered liberal terms. At this time residential development, spreading north from Shields Road, ended at Stannington Avenue on one side of Heaton Road and Cardigan Terrace on the other side.

Alderman W.H. Dunn of Gateshead was the architect of a church in the early Gothic style, with seats for 750 worshippers. Built in red brick with stone facings and mouldings, the church opened in 1897. It stands between Mundella Terrace and Balmoral Terrace.

The photograph dates from the very early 1900s, by which time residential development had reached the Meldon Terrace area in the distance. The land with trees on the left belonged to Heaton Hall which survived until 1933.

In recent years a large community building, the HBC Life Centre, has replaced the original hall at the Balmoral Terrace entrance.

13. Mundella Terrace, around 1910

MUNDELLA TERRACE, HEATON.

This view along Mundella Terrace was taken near its junction with Heaton Road. The building to the left of the photograph belongs to Heaton Baptist Church. At this time these homes were about 15 years old and residents included engineers, plumbers, clerks, foremen, tobacconists and a book binder. All the iron railings and most of the dormer windows have now disappeared.

The terrace was named after the Right Hon. A.J. Mundella, a Liberal MP for Sheffield who served under Prime Minister W.E. Gladstone with special regard for education. Mundella was responsible for an Act of Parliament in 1880, which made it compulsory for children aged between 5 and 13 to attend school though there were many exemptions for children over 10. The Act was difficult to enforce because of the lack of schools, a growing population and the tendency of parents to dodge the 'school board man' so they could send their offspring to work. An earlier Act had forbidden the employment of children under 10 and those aged between 10 and 13 who were not proficient in the three Rs but it was not entirely effective.

Mundella visited Newcastle in 1884 to open the new Liberal Club at Park Road in Elswick. The club had a reading room, smoke and games rooms, a library and a billiard room. Mundella later served as President of the Board of Trade under both W.E. Gladstone and the Earl of Rosebery.

14. Heaton Hall

Heaton Hall was originally built of brick in 1713, probably on the site of an earlier building, as the country residence of Richard Ridley a wealthy Newcastle merchant living on the Quayside. Although described at that time as 'a sweet commodious seat', it was also conveniently situated near several large collieries that belonged to the Ridley family.

The elegant appearance of the Hall in the late Victorian photograph opposite is due to a descendant, the first Sir Matthew White Ridley, who employed the well-known Newcastle architect, William Newton, to upgrade the building in the late 1770s. In particular he re-faced the front of the mansion with stone, complete with a crenellated parapet and added two battlemented corner towers plus a stylish portico.

Richard Ridley's father, Nicholas, had arrived in Newcastle from his Northumbrian home near Bardon Mill where the family had prospered for several generations. An ambitious young man, he became a successful Merchant Adventurer and acquired a considerable fortune, some of which he used to purchase a large area of land at Heaton. Nicholas also achieved high public office in Newcastle, initially as Sheriff and twice as Mayor. Bishop Nicholas Ridley, an ancestor of the family and also of Northumbrian birth, became a national martyr in 1555 at Oxford when he was burned at the stake (fastened back to back with another bishop) for his heretic protestant opinions.

In 1840, Heaton Hall was sold to Addison Langhorn Potter, a local brewer and maltster, following the

Ridley family's move to Blagdon Hall. In 1871 nine members of the Potter family were living at Heaton Hall along with 11 staff including a butler, cook, nursery governess, two nurses and six domestics. The Potter family continued to live at the Hall until 1931.

Heaton Hall was demolished in 1933 and replaced by housing in the vicinity of Heaton Park View East and Tintern Crescent.

Some of Heaton's original streets (many now demolished) had names associated with the Potter and Ridley families: Addison, Langhorn, Potter, Charles, Molineux, Matthew, Elizabeth and Stannington.

15. Holmside Place and Kingsley Place

Both of these photographs, taken in 1911, look towards Heaton Park View from Wandsworth Road. These brick houses date from the late 1880s and little has changed except that the metal railings have disappeared and some dormer attics have been created. The paved areas with metal bollards at each end remain and electric lighting has superseded gas.

The lower photograph features Kingsley Place with the Victoria Library on Heaton Park View appearing to block the far end. Holmside Place (upper picture) runs parallel to Kingsley Place with the trees of Heaton Park visible in the distance.

16. The Armstrong Gun, Heaton Park

This Armstrong gun was photographed around 1910 on a prominent site probably somewhere near the Temple. Armstrong Bridge can be seen in the middle distance together with St George's Church tower on the horizon. To the left are some of the houses of Lansdowne Gardens area in South Jesmond.

17. The Temple, Heaton Park

While upgrading Heaton Hall for the first Sir Matthew White Ridley in the 1770s, the talented local architect William Newton also designed this circular temple-like building to stand in the spacious grounds as a garden rotunda. It is said to have been a gift from Sir Matthew's tenants and friends.

After Heaton Park opened to the public in 1879, the temple functioned as a bandstand for over 50 years until it was removed to Blagdon Hall, the principal home of the Ridleys, following the demolition of Heaton Hall in 1933. It continues to stand, albeit roofless, at Blagdon by the side of a lake.

Both photographs date to the very early 1900s. The upper picture highlights one of the two curved flights of stone steps. The lower postcard features the temple together with a rear view of the nearby Victoria Library.

No. 95   The Temple Steps Heaton Park, N'C-on-Tyne.

The Temple, Heaton Park, Newcastle-on-Tyne   Valentine's Ser
H. Denholm Brash, Bookseller and Stationer, Newcastle on T

18. Victoria Library, Heaton Park View

This substantial three storey building near the southern entrance to Heaton Park opened in 1898 as 'the Victoria Library' in commemoration of Queen Victoria's Diamond Jubilee. The building, pictured here in around 1910, was the gift of Sir William Haswell Stephenson, a Tyneside industrialist, Methodist preacher and local politician, who served seven times as (Lord) Mayor of Newcastle.

Alderman Stephenson had previously paid for a library near his home at Elswick in 1893 and then decided to provide the same facility for the people of Heaton and Byker. It is said that the gift of these two libraries saved the city £15,000. In 1908 Stephenson funded a third public library at Walker. All three libraries were designed by the same architect, J.W. Dyson.

In the early years of public libraries silence was strictly enforced and the public were not allowed to browse through books – the stock was kept under lock and key and books only issued on request. Other facilities at this time included a men's reading room (standing only) as well as a separate ladies' reading room presumably with seats. Children were excluded from the adult library and had to select books from a list in a display case – if you did not like what you received from the librarian you were not allowed a second choice unless the librarian happened to be kind-hearted!

In 2000 the East End Library on Shields Road replaced Heaton Library. After more than a decade of closure, the Victorian building is now part of a mixed use development.

Free Library, Heaton, Newcastle-on-Tyne.

19. Garden Cottage, Heaton Park View

Originally known as Heaton Garden Cottage, it once stood at the entrance to Heaton Park beside the corner of Heaton Park View and Heaton Park Road. It housed the Park Constable and was probably built around 1880, shortly after the park was dedicated for public use. This photograph must have been taken after 1909 when the present tall decorative iron gates were erected on substantial 3m stone piers to celebrate the 30th anniversary of the park's opening. The date 1909 has been integrated into the wrought iron work of the gates.

The iron railings were removed during the Second World War and the cottage was demolished during the 1960s to create space for a library extension and additional car parking.

The former library and extension have now been converted into a 'mixed use development' called Victoria Buildings.

20. No. 190 Heaton Park Road

This imposing and substantial looking double-fronted house in Heaton Park Road, near to the entrance to Heaton Park, was built around 1892 for a photographer who had premises in Newcastle city centre.

In the 1901 Census the immediate neighbours in this row of well-built two-storey terrace houses included a physician/surgeon, headmaster, master builder and the vicar of nearby St Silas Church.

In the 1911 census May Geves (of private means) is head of the household at 190. She was a widow aged 36. Living with her were her children Paul, aged 18, an apprentice at a lead manufacturer's office; Francis, 13, a schoolboy; and Nora, 11, a schoolgirl. The children on the balcony are probably Francis and Nora.

Today, though looking substantially the same as it did when this photograph was taken in 1910, the house has lost its balcony (with decorative ironwork) and some of the windows have been altered. The building is now divided into flats.

21. Burnville

This 1910 photograph was taken near the junction of Ouseburn Road, in the foreground, and Stratford Road disappearing uphill. Ouseburn Road continues on to the right following the course of the Ouseburn.

Burnville on the left consisted originally of ten semi-detached brick houses built in the mid 1880s with most of them overlooking the Ouseburn. Some of these Victorian buildings have been replaced by modern dwellings. At the time of this photograph, occupants included an oil merchant, two bricklayers and a couple of mariners.

The semi-detached houses on the other side of Stratford Road date to around 1890 and remain intact. Residents around 1910 included a grocer, fishmonger and a naturalist.

This area is no longer a tranquil part of Heaton. Stratford Road is particularly busy with traffic and is on a bus route.

22. The Lake, Heaton Park

Beyond the croquet ground and the bowling green was the lake 'Where swans and water fowl of various kinds, swim fearlessly up to bystanders and look up to be fed'. The lake, with a small island near its centre, was part of the original Heaton Hall Estate, and was similar in size to the bowling green.

The photograph below is facing the terrace and pavilion with the edge of the lake on the left. Maggie's note on the postcard reminds us of the time, before instant communication, when friends would write to each other knowing that there were at least two postal deliveries each day.

To the left of the upper postcard, surprisingly, can be seen a small circular bear pit surrounded by iron railings (a colour reproduction is on page 10). It's tempting to think that the bear's head is just visible reaching for a change of diet dangling from a nearby tree.

The lake was replaced by shrubs and trees during the 1930s and a concrete paddling pool opened downhill near the junction of Ouseburn Road and Jesmond Vale Lane. The paddling pool, still there, but derelict, superseded an area previously used for playing quoits.

NEWCASTLE-ON-TYNE.-HEATON PARK.

28/04 Bring Isabell's smock. pinnies & Dresses with you to day Maggie

23. Bowling Green and Pavilion, Heaton Park

This photograph, probably dating to around 1890, features the original bowling green and a wooden pavilion belonging to the Armstrong Bowling Club that adjoined the croquet ground.

Near the east (or left side of the pavilion) was a circular pit with a central climbing pole that for many years contained a large brown bear, which danced with a cane and ate buns (see previous page). The pit, surrounded by iron railings, was only large enough for one animal and was removed during the early 1900s to be replaced by shrubbery.

In 1913 the wooden pavilion was deliberately set alight by militant suffragettes who left a note nearby saying 'No Peace Until Votes for Women'. The pavilion and the open fronted shelter in front of it were ruined beyond repair causing much distress to members, many of whom lost their bowls and clothing in the blaze. There was no loss of life because the fire was started around midnight when the park gates would have been locked. Later that year, Emily Wilding Davison, a prominent suffragette and a Northumbrian by birth, threw herself under the King's horse on Derby Day, died of her injuries and lies buried in St Mary's Churchyard at Morpeth.

Most of the area covered by the bowling green and pavilion has now been landscaped with shrubs, trees and paths following the transfer of the bowling green to the site of the former croquet ground.

The New Bowling Green, Heaton Park, Newcastle.

24. The Pavilion, Terrace and Greens, Heaton Park

Heaton Park Pavilion originated in 1884 as an aviary containing a selection of colourful, exotic birds including an eagle. Also on display were a raccoon and several monkeys. The pavilion and adjoining hot-houses were built on a broad terrace, fronted by a stone balustrade with wide steps leading down to a croquet lawn and beyond to an adjoining bowling green together with its own, much smaller, pavilion.

The pavilion was later extended to provide a shelter, a café and other facilities. A large fountain was recycled from an earlier life in Newcastle's Grainger Market, but didn't function as a working fountain here. Four Armstrong Field Guns were an added attraction on the terrace (see the colour postcard on page 10).

This photograph, taken around 1890, shows the original aviary together with the croquet lawn and part of the bowling green to the left. The pear tree alongside the bowling green continues to flourish.

Fire badly damaged the pavilion, aviary and terrace in 1979. Surviving ironwork was restored at Beamish Museum before being returned as part of a major restoration scheme. The Victorian building was recreated by using handmade yellowed bricks and painting the ironwork with typical 19th century shades of dark red, black, cream and olive. The re-vamped pavilion, terrace and park were re-opened in 1984 and shortly afterwards won a Civic Trust Award.

Today a bowling green has replaced the croquet lawn. The original bowling green and pavilion have become an area of shrubs and trees. The fountain and guns no longer grace the terrace.

Walk 3 Chillingham Rd and the Avenues (linear).

By 1899 most houses in this part of Heaton as far north as Rothbury Terrace had been built. The area to the north of Rothbury Terrace was still largely rural with more streets planned for the very near future. Heaton Farm still survived just east of Jesmond Vale Terrace.

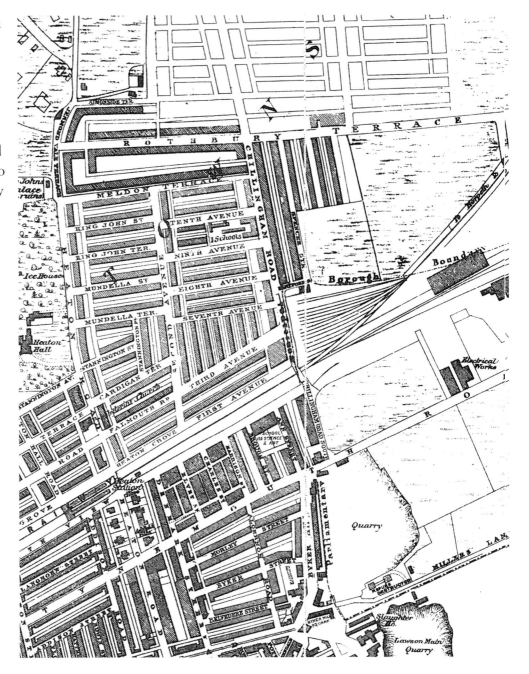

1. Lord Clyde Hotel
2. Ringtons Ltd.
3. St Mark's Church
4. Chillingham Road South
5. Shields Road East
6. C.A. Parsons & Co.
7. F. Turnbull & Co.
8. North View School
9. The Chillingham
10. Fifth Avenue
11. Jack Common, Third Avenue
12. Guildford Place and Cheltenham Terrace
13. Brough's Store
14. Presbyterian Church
15. Heaton Road shops
16. Heaton Road shops
17. Chas Chandler, Second Avenue
18. Heaton Junction Sports Ground
19. Chillingham Road School

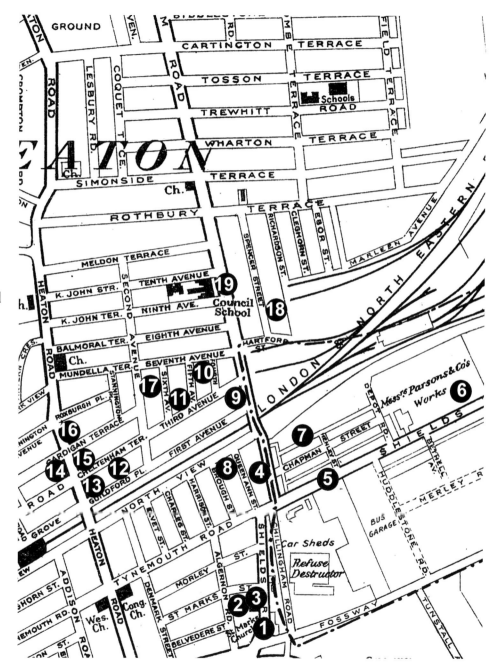

1. Lord Clyde Hotel

Initially known as The Fox and Hounds at Byker Hill (now Shields Road), its origins go back to at least 1849. The name was changed to the Lord Clyde Hotel during the mid 1860s in memory of Sir Colin Campbell, hero of the Indian Mutiny. A Glaswegian by birth, he was raised to the peerage a few years before his death in 1863. He commanded the Highland Brigade at Balaclava during the Crimean War and later, as Commander in Chief of the Indian Army, he successfully raised the siege of Lucknow and Cawnpore during the Mutiny.

The Lord Clyde Hotel was rebuilt in 1896 to the design of the popular local architect Benjamin F. Simpson for the owners and brewers John Rowell & Sons of Gateshead. Newcastle Breweries took over the premises in the mid 1950s. The photograph is dated 1966.

Today the pub is known as Peggy Sue's Bar. A rear entrance (for goods) in Algernon Road retains 'Lord Clyde Hotel' on a lintel over a gateway.

2. Ringtons Ltd., 1967

This impressive five-storey purpose-built tea blending factory belonging to Ringtons Ltd was opened at Algernon Road in 1926.

There was never a Mr Rington. The name is formed from the surnames of both founders of the business namely, William Titterington and Samuel Smith. The letter S is intended to represent Smith so the name of the business is written without an apostrophe.

Samuel Smith (1872-1949) OBE JP was born in Leeds. Coming from humble origins, he began work aged about 10 as an errand boy with a firm of tea merchants. He rose through the ranks to become a senior sales executive by the age of 35.

Smith had a vision of selling tea from door to door from attractively liveried horse-drawn vans but because of a restrictive covenant was unable to achieve this dream in Yorkshire. In 1907 he resigned his position in Leeds and moved to Newcastle with his

family of six young children. He lived for a while in Third Avenue, Heaton, rented a nearby 'lock-up' and formed a partnership with William Titterington. It seems as though Titterington provided the initial finance for a horse, van, utensils and a stock of tea. Within a few years Smith was able to repay Titterington's investment and then ran the company business by himself.

In 1992 a new factory for tea blending and coffee roasting opened at Longbenton and the Algernon Road factory was taken over by a firm of auctioneers and valuers. A 1963 double-storey brick extension to the Algernon Road property is still in use as the company's head office and warehousing space. Door-to-door deliveries continue to cover the northern counties of England plus parts of Lincolnshire, Nottinghamshire and Scotland.

3. St Mark's Church, Shields Road, 1930

St Mark's Church was consecrated in 1906 and stands on that part of Shields Road formerly known as Byker Hill. It was the third church to be formed out of the adjacent and densely crowded parish of St Michael's at Byker – the other churches were St Silas (1886) and St Gabriel's (1899).

The present building replaced a temporary iron structure and was designed by Hicks and Charlewood in a 15th century style with seats for 800 people. Construction took two years and the cost (£15,000) was met by William Donaldson Cruddas, a prominent Newcastle businessman and former MP who lived at Elswick. Cruddas had previously contributed generously to the construction of St Stephen's Church at Elswick as well as donating land for the Cruddas Recreation Ground.

St Mark's Church was deconsecrated following a large scale redevelopment of the area. It is now the Newcastle Climbing Centre with over 1200 square metres of climbing walls for roped climbing and bouldering.

Cruddas also financed the buildings on either side of the church. To the left was the parish hall completed in 1911 (the foundation stone can still be seen) and to the right was the vicarage (not on this photograph), which is now the business premises of a funeral director.

4. Chillingham Road South and Chapman Street, 1972

Today this scene is almost unrecognisable. All the houses, including Chapman Street, have been demolished. The dwellings on the right have been replaced by a deep cutting for the Metro line between Byker and Chillingham Road. The entrance to Chillingham Road Metro Station is near the 'skew' railway bridge over the main east coast railway line on the left of the picture.

Chapman Street, on the right, at one time a short cut for some employees working at nearby Parsons engineering works, is probably named after William Chapman (1749-1832) who was a civil engineer. One of his earliest patents enabled coal to be lowered into the holds of collier vessels in wagons, instead of being sent down chutes which broke and damaged the coal.

Chapman was also involved in the pioneering work of locomotive development and one of his engines was used on the Heaton Colliery Waggonway from 1813. The development of the bogie, a pivoting undercarriage to enable locomotives to negotiate curves in the waggonways, appears to have been due largely to Chapman's ingenuity.

5. Shields Road East

This photograph was taken in around 1901, maybe at the end of a working day, looking east along Shields Road from the Byker Hill area. Recently built Tyneside flats are visible on the left, on either side of the Henley Street junction. Just beyond the terrace of dwellings is the low slanting roof of Charles Parsons' engineering workshop where most of these cloth capped men probably worked. Beyond, in the gloom, are the double-storey company offices, complete with chimney stacks. The tall building on the right is part of the tram sheds belonging to Newcastle Corporation.

The photograph below, taken from a similar position, is dated nearly 80 years later. While the houses and tram (now bus) sheds remain, a six-storey office block can be seen on the left towering over homes. This office block, built for C.A. Parsons and Co., replaced the Victorian workshop and offices in the 1950s.

Most of these buildings have now disappeared. A light industrial estate has replaced housing on the left side of the road while a large retail park has transformed the opposite side. The tall office block has been demolished and the site awaits redevelopment. Beyond the office block is the lofty machine shop once belonging to Parsons but now owned by their former European rival, Siemens.

6. C.A. Parsons & Co. Ltd.

From a very early age Charles Algernon Parsons was interested in all things mechanical, making models, handling tools, and above all devising experiments to test his ideas. His father was a distinguished engineer and astronomer so Charles must have had a thorough grounding in science. Born in London, Charles served a successful engineering apprenticeship at the Elswick Works of Sir William Armstrong.

After working for a few engineering companies he established his own works in 1889, aged 35, on a two acre site (the size of a football pitch) near Heaton Junction. With a staff of 48 he began to manufacture steam turbines, dynamos and other electrical machinery. The original site was immediately east of the Shields Road junction with Depot Road. By 1900 the works had more than quadrupled in size and sixty years later there were about 8,000 employees working on a sixty acre site.

Of Parsons' many inventions and over 300 patents, the steam turbine (patented 1884) is perhaps the most important. He developed its use world wide for the generation of electricity in power stations. The first power station in the world to employ this revolutionary turbo generating plant was here in Newcastle in 1890 at Forth Banks.

Above, a typical manufactured component, 1956.

Right, Parsons', 1971.

In 1894 Parsons turned his attention to the need for more efficient marine propulsion and developed *Turbinia*, the world's first turbine powered vessel. One of Charles' proudest moments must have been when, in order to get Admiralty recognition for his invention, he piloted the tiny *Turbinia* among the fleet of international warships assembled off the Isle of Wight for the Naval Review to celebrate the Diamond Jubilee of Queen Victoria in 1897.

Later, the steam turbine was used to power passenger liners, one of which, the Blue Riband for the fastest crossing of the Atlantic, the locally built *Mauretania* (1906), held for over 20 years. The original *Turbinia* is at the Discovery Museum in Newcastle.

Considered by some as the most original engineer since James Watt, Parsons was showered with honours and awards including fellow of the Royal Society 1898, a knighthood in 1911 and the Order of Merit in 1927. He was the first engineer to win this honour.

Parsons died in 1931, aged 76, while on holiday in the Caribbean and is buried at Kirkwhelpington, Northumberland. His estate was worth over a million pounds.

7. F. Turnbull & Co., Heaton Junction

A much smaller, but successful, engineering firm at Heaton Junction was F. Turnbull & Co. (Engineers) Ltd. who were tucked in near Parsons at Heaton Junction with an address at Back Chapman Street. The cast iron drain covers made by this small foundry can still be seen all over Newcastle bearing the firm's name and address. The firm also made the castings for the rivets that hold the Tyne Bridge together. Fred Turnbull, who established the firm in 1910, lived for several years at No. 2 Stannington Grove, with his wife Annie and daughters Marjorie, Gracie and May (they attended Chillingham Road School). The firm continued as a family-run business until the 1960s.

MUNICIPAL CASTINGS

MANHOLE COVERS
AND ROAD GULLIES
FOR ALL PURPOSES

F. TURNBULL & CO. (Engineers) LTD.
HEATON JUNCTION   NEWCASTLE-ON-TYNE, 6
Telegrams STANCHION Newcastle.   Telephone Newcastle 656037

8. North View School

This photograph of North View, taken in about 1974, looks towards Chillingham Road with part of the former Metal Box Company's building just visible. In the centre is North View School with a prominent 'bell turret' on the roof and to the left below the trees and out of sight is the railway.

This two-storey school, built of brick, opened in 1892. Designed by Mr D. Campbell, it catered for about 950 pupils. The school was unusual at this time because the curriculum included science and the arts as well as the usual elementary subjects. The reason for this was that in nearby Heaton Road there was already a Science and Art School (begun by the well known local educationalist Dr J.H. Rutherford) operating in a large villa. It became so popular it could not take all the pupils who wished to attend. When the new Board School was at the planning stage provision was made to include extra facilities such as a laboratory and lecture room, a photographic developing room and a cookery room.

The school closed in the early 1980s and has been replaced by purpose-built sheltered accommodation (Northfields House). Low-rise terraced housing now covers the surrounding area.

9. The Chillingham, Chillingham Road, 1966

The Chillingham pub stands on Chillingham Road between the railway and Third Avenue, the corner of which is just visible to the right of the photograph. The building opened as the East End Hotel in around 1893, at a time when most of the surrounding houses were newly built. The adjacent railway marshalling yards were in full swing, the cricket and football grounds were close by and Heaton Railway Station was not too far away. The hotel offered spacious rooms for dancing, dinners and parties, a bar, a luxuriously fitted buffet and smoking and billiard rooms.

Initially there had been much opposition to the hotel from the Temperance Movement and some churches that saw licensed premises as 'a temptation placed in the way of the young and to those who passed by'.

In 1907 the name was changed to the Chillingham Hotel. About 30 years later it was rebuilt. Today the pub is simply known as the Chillingham or just the Chilli!

Behind The Chillingham, with an entrance in First Avenue is the Meadowfield Social Club. It stands on the site of a much older dwelling in its own grounds that dated back to at least 1870. Known as Meadow Field House, in 1871 it was the home of a brick and tile manufacturer. Later in the century it became the residence of the Turnbull family, Newcastle innkeepers whose properties included the East End Hotel.

10. Fifth Avenue

Fifth Avenue is photographed here before and after a face lift 1969-70. Before this date many of the front gardens were overgrown, untidy and neglected with a variety of makeshift fences that replaced iron railings removed during the Second World War. A study on the revitalisation of the area suggested that more should be made of open space, trees should be planted and stonework repaired.

Both photographs look towards Seventh Avenue. Over the rooftops of the opposite photo can be seen St Gabriel's Church tower, the Spinney multi storey flats and the roofline of Chillingham Road Schools with their tall, attractive chimneys.

The Avenues, as they are often referred to, were built during the early to mid 1890s following the sale of land by the Meadowfield Estate to various speculative builders who became landlords. These Tyneside Flats, with twin front doors were popular with local workers and consisted of either an

'upstairs' (4 rooms) or a 'downstairs' (3 rooms) with each flat having a kitchen, sometimes with a bath. The small back yard contained the earth closets and coal houses. A planned road in front of the houses was deferred (and never built) meanwhile front gardens were created to help fill the space and tenants were asked to pay an annual charge of 6d to the local authority.

The properties were modernised over the years, with inside toilets, the installation of electricity and improved water supplies. Fourth and Sixth avenues, on either side of Fifth Avenue were not included in the renovation of 1969-1970 and have kept their front gardens.

11. Jack Common (1903-1968) Novelist

John William Common, the son of an engine driver, was born in 1903 in an upstairs Tyneside flat at 44 Third Avenue near Heaton railway junction. A commemorative plaque marks the house.

At the age of 14 Jack left Chillingham Road School with an average academic record, except for an obvious talent in essay writing, first to attend commercial college and then find employment in a solicitor's office.

In an attempt to seek more suitable and permanent work, Common moved to London but found it equally difficult and was only able to obtain casual work as varied as a mechanic, a script writer, a labourer and an assistant magazine editor. During this period he met George Orwell, who became his friend and mentor and who, now and again, found it necessary to offer financial assistance to the Tynesider. Orwell regarded Common as 'the most genuine proletarian voice in Britain'.

At the age of 48, Common's first and best known novel, *Kiddar's Luck*, was published. It was based on his difficult upbringing as a child of a broken marriage in Edwardian Newcastle. A few years later his other book *The Ampersand* appeared. It looked at life in Newcastle after leaving school. Neither book was a commercial success and Common lived in poverty for much of the rest of his life.

Common died of lung cancer at Newport Pagnall, aged 64. Many of his diaries and letters are preserved at the Robinson Library, Newcastle University.

Jack Common House, built in 1994, is at the corner of Mundella Terrace and Heaton Road. It contains 31 flats with support and a wide range of facilities for older people.

Opposite, a view of the Avenues around 1996. The Tyneside flats of the Avenues were completed in the 1890s.

Chillingham Road

Second Avenue

83

12. The bombing of Guildford Place and Cheltenham Terrace, 1941

For a few minutes during the evening of 25 April 1941, Heaton was the subject of a devastating air raid by the German Luftwaffe. Nine high explosive bombs, a powerful parachute mine and a host of incendiary bombs were dropped and 47 men, women and children died as a result of the raid, with a further

ncjMedia

70 injured. Some were badly disabled. Sixteen houses and shops were demolished and a further 300 were damaged.

Most of the deaths and structural damage occurred at Guildford Place and nearby Cheltenham Terrace, as a direct result of the powerful land-mine that was intended to destroy the adjacent railway. The majority of residents remained inside their homes, completely unaware of how much danger they were in until some people heard the whoosh of the parachute mine as it neared the ground. At this point it was too late to take precautions. Later, a survivor recalled that the explosion was as if 'someone had discharged a rifle an inch from your ear'.

The photograph was taken in Guildford Place the following day. It took several days to clear up the debris and recover bodies for burial. The remains of unidentified victims were interred at Byker and Heaton Cemetery in a common grave.

Three-storey flats in both Guildford Place and Cheltenham Terrace now cover the site.

13. Brough's Store

It's hard to imagine how so many members of staff could ever have worked efficiently in such a relatively small shop. The photograph dates from around 1924 and may well have marked Brough's occupation of the premises in that year. Built around 1897, the shop still stands on Heaton Road at the corner of Guildford Place (next to the railway) and is now known as the Heaton Village Store.

Edward Brough, the founder of the business and an American by birth, arrived on Tyneside in 1848 at the age of two and remained here for the rest of his long life. After working for many years in the wholesale grocery business, he and his son set up a retail grocery business in 1888, with the object of lowering the price of goods to customers by buying in bulk and by cutting out the middleman. The business prospered with many branches throughout the region and in 1917 had over 500 employees.

The Broughs were generous to local charities, particularly the Poor Children's Holiday Association. They donated a house in Whickham to be used as the Edith Brough Children's Home. Edward made various charitable bequests in his will as well as leaving one year's wages to each of his staff who were in employment for at least a year before his death.

14. The Presbyterian Church, Heaton Road

The Presbyterian Church buildings pictured here in 1910 stood on Heaton Road between Cardigan Terrace (leading off to the right) and Falmouth Road, just visible behind the church's very tall turret.

At this time the church was comprised of two separate buildings. The single-storey church hall in the foreground opened in 1891, with seats for 500 people, classrooms and a house for the church officer. Five years later, a more substantial church with an 88ft polygonal turret opened. It had seats for 800 people and was the first church in Heaton to be lit by electricity. Newcastle architect W.L. Newcombe designed the church. The cost of both buildings amounted to £8,300.

Today, the church is known as St Cuthbert's Church, a United Reform and Methodist Partnership and has been relocated to the former church hall. The original church was demolished and replaced by several flats known as Alison Court.

In the early days Presbyterians in Newcastle's East End rented various buildings until, in 1881, they built their first church in nearby Denmark Street before moving to the Heaton Road site. Regular Bible readings take place in what is now known as Denmark Street Hall.

15. Heaton Road shops

This row of shops, built around 1895, had the luxury of a street lamp outside each of the seven businesses between Cheltenham Terrace and Cardigan Terrace (further away). In the far distance are the trees in the grounds of Heaton Hall. The single deck tram car is heading to the terminus at Simonside Terrace.

When this photograph was taken in around 1903, the shops were, from right to left, a bakery, a stationers (note the 'Heaton Circulating Library and Book Store', second shop from the right), a grocer, an ironmonger, a fruiterer, a tobacconist and a draper. Today the buildings house a confectioner, a power tool firm and an office dealing with student lettings.

16. Heaton Road shops

A sunny day on Heaton Road in around 1910, looking towards Shields Road in the distance from the Stannington Avenue junction.

The nearest building on the right is the former Co-operative grocery store, which opened in 1892 and is now divided into commercial units. Next is the one-time Presbyterian Church with its impressive tower and in the background is the lofty tower of the Cuthbert Bainbridge Memorial Methodist Chapel.

The other side of Heaton Road is dominated by nearly 30 shops and businesses. Many food shops are represented in addition to an ironmonger, a hosier and glover, a post office and a branch of the London City and Midland Bank. Today, the businesses include a sandwich bar, a delicatessen, a tanning studio, a launderette and no less than four businesses dealing with student lettings, but no post office or bank.

No. 92   Heaton Road, N C-on-Tyne.

17. Second Avenue: Chas Chandler (1938-1996) – Musician, producer, manager

Chas Chandler (real name Brian James Chandler) spent the first 25 years of his life at 35 Second Avenue, Heaton. This giant of a man (6ft 4in tall) with endless enthusiasm and drive worked initially in the shipyards as a turner before joining the Alan Price trio in his early 20s as bass guitarist. Re-named 'The Animals', this rock group was based at the Club A'Go Go in Percy Street (above the former Handyside's Arcade). They also toured extensively.

The Animals disbanded in 1966 and Chandler, tired of non-stop travelling for three years, decided to try his hand at managing potential star musicians, a switch that few others were able to achieve. He first of all spotted and then managed the American guitarist Jimi Hendrix (formerly Jimmy Jones) and produced all his hit singles, including *Hey Joe*, between 1966 and 1968. In the 1970s Chandler transformed the Wolverhampton rock band Slade into one of the most prolific hit makers of the decade.

In later life Chandler operated a recording studio where he developed his own record label (Barn Records). He was part owner of the Newcastle Arena, a large sports and entertainment complex with seats for 10,000 people. Sadly Chandler died of a heart condition in 1996, aged 57.

Jim Perry

The Alan Price Combo, with the 6ft 4ins Chas Chandler central on guitar, around 1962.

18. Heaton Junction Sports Ground

In the late 1870s Heaton Cricket Club became the first occupant of a former eight-acre rectangular field at the east side of Chillingham Road next to Heaton Junction railway sidings and soon after, one of Tyneside's earliest football clubs, North Eastern (formed from the workers of the North Eastern Railway Company) played alongside. Another, more important football club followed a few years later. The ground was also used for athletics and had a bicycle track. The cricket field adjoined Rothbury Terrace to the north, while the football pitch bordered the railway sidings to the south. Financial problems led to the club's demise in 1885 and the following year the ground was taken over by the East End Football Club.

The East End Football Club had originated as an offshoot of the Stanley Cricket Club and originally played on a field near Stanley Street in the St Peter's area of south Byker. Later the club moved to a more accessible ground near Dalton Street, also in Byker, and changed their name to the East End Football Club. In 1886 the club moved to the Heaton Junction ground where there were better facilities.

East End Football Club became very successful at Heaton Junction and began to compete outside the region, assisted by the rapid growth of the railways. An 'imposing new stand' made of timber, was erected in the late 1880s and in the 1891-92 season the club reached the first round 'proper' of the FA Cup, only to be narrowly beaten 2-1 by Nottingham Forest. East End colours varied from season to season but just before their move to St James' Park, red jerseys became the official strip with black and white stripes, the County colours, as an alternative.

Changing accommodation at this time was often in the nearest pub. Goal nets, offside and penalty kicks were all developments for the future and not all clubs had goal posts with crossbars. Although crossbars had been introduced in 1875, some clubs continued to use 'tape between the sticks'. Local football was largely played by enthusiasts most of whom would have worked on Saturday mornings. This meant that games often had to be cut short because of travelling delays or gathering darkness during the game. It was not unusual for spectators to be asked to deputise for absent players and when referees

Victorian collector cards were popular at the time throughout the country and East End FC was featured.

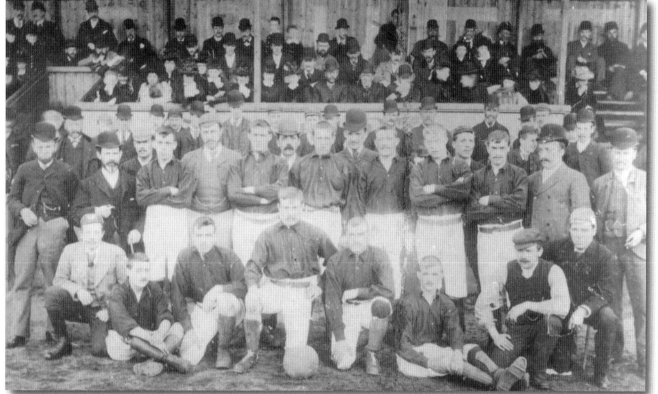

P Joannou–Newcastle United FC archive

Newcastle United's pioneers, East End FC pictured in red shirts at Chillingham Road in April 1892 just before moving base from Heaton to St James' Park.

could not be found it was left to club captains to sort out disputes.

In 1892 West End Football Club, Tyneside's other top team and arch rivals of the East End Club, had just disbanded following a series of poor results. At this point, East End were offered and accepted the opportunity to take over West End's ground at St James' Park. The new name of Newcastle United was soon adopted. The club was accepted into Division 2 of the English Football League followed in 1898 by promotion into Division 1.

The Heaton Junction ground continued to be used by other football and cricket clubs until it was replaced by housing and railway extensions from the late 1890s.

19. Chillingham Road School

Chillingham Road School and Ouseburn School were opened on the same day in 1893. They were built using the 'most modern principles' including smaller, separate classrooms. Another development involved separating the infants from the rest of the school.

Architects Oliver and Leeson designed Chillingham Road school to hold 1,100 pupils in separate buildings for juniors (800) and infants (300). Boys and girls each had their own play yard with covered areas for use in wet weather. Built of red brick with roofs of grey slate, the architecture was plain apart from the ornamental chimneys.

The school was provided with especially wide corridors 'for drilling [exercising] in'. Much consideration was given to heating and ventilation. Water screening equipment, fans and flues meant the air in the buildings could be changed every six minutes, reducing stuffiness and the spread of infectious diseases.

This photograph, dated 1966, was taken in Tenth Avenue looking towards the infants school which was on the ground floor. Overhead on the first floor were the rooms for cookery, carpentry, art and laundry classes. The caretaker's house is on the left of the photograph. Because it was almost central to the site, it had excellent all-round views of the school buildings.

The school is now a primary school.

These warmly dressed school children were photographed on the steps of the Pavilion in Heaton Park in 1898. The ornate fountain at the top of the steps was 'recycled' to Heaton Park from the Grainger Market.

Walk 4. The Peoples Theatre to Iris Brickfield Community Park (linear)

The last walk takes place in that part of Heaton, north of Rothbury Terrace, developed from 1900, although a few houses in Simonside Terrace date from an earlier period. In 1899 St Gabriel's Church was under construction, Northumberland Cricket Club was flourishing, and the remains of Middle Pit (far right) are still marked on this map.

The large plots marked out for villas to the left of Heaton Road (opposite the cricket ground) were never built. Instead semi-villas were constructed in the 1920s and 1930s. To the east of Heaton Road the eventual street layout bears some resemblance to the initial plans shown here.

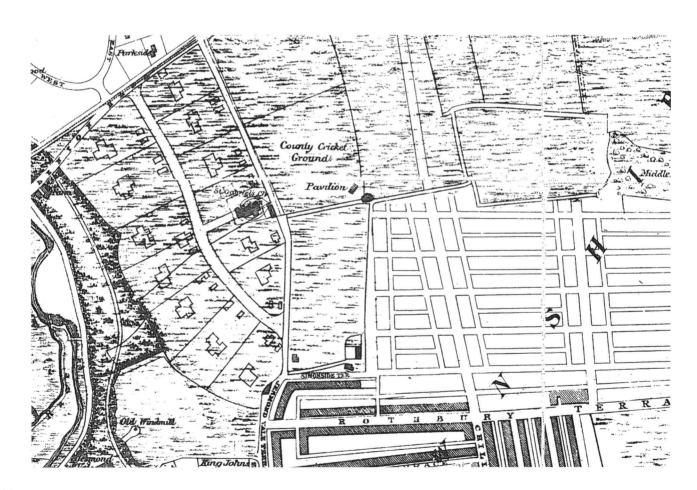

1. People's Theatre (Lyric Cinema)

2. Corner House Hotel

3. Northumberland Cricket Club Ground

4. St Gabriel's Church

5. Heaton Methodist Church

6. Jesmond Vale Terrace

7. Coquet Terrace

8. Chillingham Road - Trewhitt Road junction

9. Scala Cinema

10. Chillingham Road - Cartington Terrace junction

11. St Gabriel's Parish Hall

12. Heaton Pool

13. North Heaton Council Schools

14. Iris Brickfield Community Park

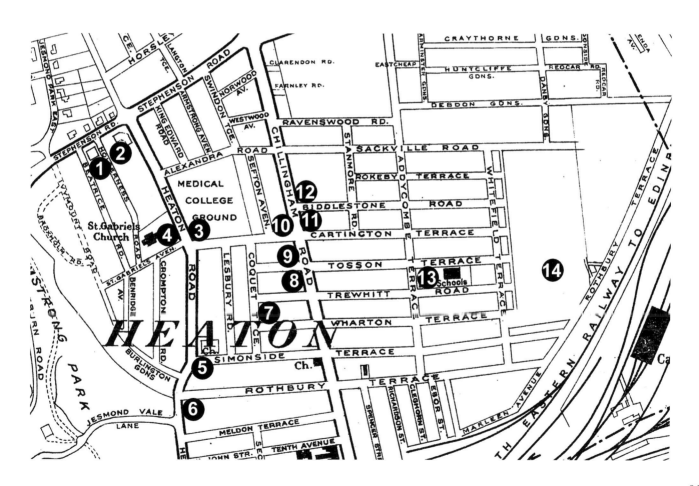

1. Lyric Cinema, Stephenson Road

With a cutting edge in construction, decoration, furnishings and equipment, the Lyric opened as a 'super' cinema in 1936. Marshall and Tweedy were the architects. Built in brick, it accommodated 1,594 viewers in attractive, padded seats in an auditorium (decorated mainly in pink) where horizontal bands of black and silver gave a three-dimensional effect, 'as if the walls were completely cushioned all round'. Much was made of an integral café that opened for 12 hours a day to cater for locals and people visiting the nearby public parks. There was a large car park for patrons behind the cinema. Because the Lyric and the Apollo on Shields Road had the same owner, economies were made by using a page-boy to carry the film between the two cinemas on a bicycle, a distance of about a mile.

The cinema closed in 1959 and the building was acquired by the People's Theatre Arts Group for £27,000. After some alterations, the theatre opened in 1962 with a production of *Man and Superman* by G.B. Shaw. The People's began in 1911 as 'The Clarion Dramatic Club' in an upstairs room at the corner of Percy Street and Leazes Park Road before moving four years later to the Royal Arcade, during which time it became known as The People's Theatre. From 1930 until 1962 the theatre functioned at Rye Hill in a former non-conformist chapel until their move to Heaton, where they still flourish today.

2. Corner House Hotel, Stephenson Road

When the Corner House Hotel opened in 1936, it was only the second public house built in Heaton since the early 1870s. There had been considerable opposition to the hotel on the grounds of its likely effect on school children and a local Methodist church regarded its construction as 'immoral'. Many feared Heaton Road would become a 'bear garden'. However the vicar of nearby St Gabriel's fully supported the scheme on the grounds that it was too far for him to travel to the Chillingham Hotel (about one mile away and the first pub to be built after the 1870s) to buy beer and his congregation 'certainly desired' licensed premises in the vicinity.

Local brewer James Deuchar, engaged architects Marshall and Tweedy to design the hotel in a 'charming quaint Dutch style'. It opened a few days after the Lyric Cinema only a few yards away. Not only were the public house facilities of the highest quality but included a commodious dining room, five well-appointed bedrooms with hot and cold water, oak panelling in all rooms and full central heating. Outside they planned to have a bowling green, a lawn, space for 100 cars and a wine shop.

One of the most popular beers at the Corner House was Lochside, named after the steamer that carried the barrels on a 16-hour voyage from Deuchar's brewery at Montrose. Some patrons insisted the beer tasted better after stormy weather at sea.

3. Former Northumberland Cricket Club Ground

When this cricket ground opened in 1881 as the new home of the Northumberland Cricket Club, it was remote and surrounded by fields and meadows. For over 40 years previously the club had played their matches at Bath Road (now Northumberland Road) but because of projected building developments in that area, it had been forced to seek alternative accommodation.

It was at this point that Sir W.G. Armstrong made an offer to the club of a 6 acre field in Heaton Lane (now road) at a nominal rent as part of a 10 year lease. A cricket square was prepared and a pavilion constructed, although the ground remained unenclosed for several years.

The Northumberland Cricket Club was a private club with no ambitions towards serious competition, but during its existence it allowed the Northumberland County Cricket Club (which had no home ground) to rent the facilities for representative and inter-county games. The Heaton Lane ground eventually proved to be anything but ideal for representative games largely due to its isolation and a lack of adequate public transport. In 1897 some influential gentlemen were able to raise sufficient funds to acquire an existing sports field at Osborne Avenue Jesmond. This venue in Jesmond became the first (and present) permanent home of the Northumberland County Cricket Club.

In 1899 the Northumberland Cricket Club folded and the ground was acquired by the College of Medicine Athletic Club. Newcastle University now uses the facilities for their sporting activities and today the ground is an oasis amid much residential development.

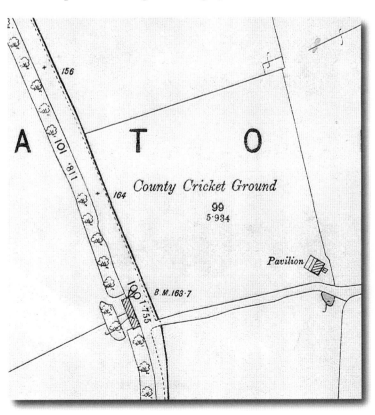

The cricket ground, reduced from the 1890 OS map. Heaton Lane was a tree-lined lane which would become Heaton Road, and the cricket ground was surrounded by fields.

4. St Gabriel's Church, Heaton Road

The consecration of St Gabriel's Church took place in 1899. The land at Heaton Road was gifted by Lord Armstrong who also, along with several others, made generous cash donations towards the estimated final cost of around £10,000. At this time the church was incomplete and consisted only of the nave, south aisle and porch. However, with the temporary chancel and vestry there was enough of it to create the new parish of St Gabriel's. It was to be another 30 years before the church was completed.

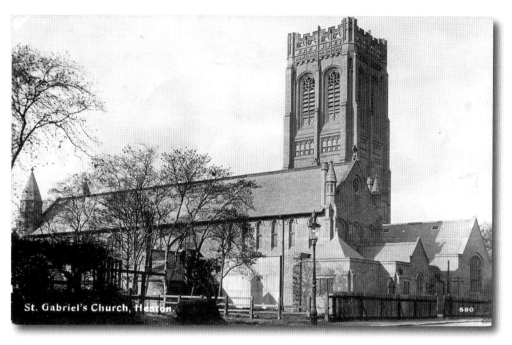

St. Gabriel's Church, Heaton.

St Gabriel's originated in1890 as a temporary iron structure in Rothbury Terrace, close to Chillingham Road (then under construction) and overlooking a cricket ground, now covered by Spencer Street and Richardson Street. It was necessary to create this 'chapel of ease' from the parish and church of St Michael's at Byker because of the ongoing population explosion in Heaton. This iron church later became St Gabriel's Parish Hall until a replacement was built further along Chillingham Road.

Architect Frank W. Rich designed the new church at Heaton Road in the English Parish Church style of the 14th century. Built with high quality sandstone, it had a spacious interior to seat 1,000. Around the upper part of the 99 feet high battlemented bell tower, is a Gothic- lettered frieze which reads : 'Holy Holy Holy Lord God Almighty, Heaven and Earth are full of your Glory'.

This photo must have been taken sometime between the building of the church hall (to the right of the tower) in 1924 and the completion of the south transept in 1931.

5. Heaton Methodist Church, around 1904

In 1899 the ambitious United Methodist Free Church, decided to leave their cramped building on Shields Road and look for a more suitable site as Heaton's residential population continued to expand northwards. A plot of land on Heaton Road at the corner of Simonside Terrace was secured and architects Maxwell and Hope were engaged to design a late Gothic style building to seat 700 people. The Shields Road church only had seats for 320.

The first part of the development to open was a school (1901), where services continued while the larger church was being built. The church opened in 1902. The total cost including land, furnishings and fittings amounted to over £10,500 and was partly financed by the sale of the Shields Road property for £6,750. 'Simonside' as the church is often known today, is the fourth site of the Society that began in 1850 as the 'Byker Hill Wesleyan Reformers' and has had several changes of name since then. Since 1932 it has officially been known as Heaton Methodist Church.

The photograph shows a class C single deck tram car No.46, about to leave the terminus on its journey back to Scotswood via Shields Road and Market Street. The church and the large semi-detached villas to its left are of similar age. Housing on the other side of Heaton Road appeared from the 1920s.

6. Jesmond Vale Terrace, Heaton Road, around 1910

One of the earliest residential developments in Heaton began in 1880 at Jesmond Vale Terrace (later to become part of Heaton Road) in a superb situation opposite the newly opened public parks. The houses had an uninterrupted view overlooking Jesmond Vale and beyond. The terrace consisted of 18 two-storey homes (with attics) using white bricks and was completed by the end of the decade.

Most of the dwellings were occupied by business and professional people. When this photograph was taken there was a ladies' seminary in one of the houses. It later developed into Heaton High School. In the 1920s and 1930s a businessman called Samuel Smith was living in the terrace. He was a founder partner of Ringtons tea merchants who later diversified into building electrical vehicles.

A blue plaque at No.16 marks the birthplace of Sir Ove Arup in 1895, founder of one of the largest and best-known structural and civil engineering partnerships in the world. The son of a Danish vet connected with the import of live cattle and sheep into the River Tyne, Ove became a consultant for many international projects. Locally he was involved with the building of the Tyneside Metro including three stations, several bridges and the award-winning Byker Viaduct (1982).

7. Coquet Terrace

The houses in Coquet Terrace date from around 1903. The photograph below was taken a few years later from near Simonside Terrace looking towards Cartington Terrace and the College of Medicine Athletic Ground. Semi-detached houses line the left side with terraced housing on the right. Occupants in around 1910 included various types of engineer, a police sergeant, a block and mast maker and a couple of schoolmasters. Lord Armstrong owned much of the land in this area so many of the streets have names associated with Northumberland.

Left, the back garden at No. 15 Coquet Terrace, 1920. At that time John Catto, a consulting marine engineer, lived there with his wife Harriet and sons Archie, Jock and Bill.

Private collection

8. Chillingham Road – Trewhitt Road junction

A general view in 1974 of part of Chillingham Road's main shopping area. The nearest junction on both sides of Chillingham Road is Trewhitt Road and in the distance is the bridge over the railway and beyond to Shields Road.

Most of the shops have changed ownership and type. For example, the firm of butchers on the right (Manners & Sons Ltd) is now a video hire shop and a pizza takeaway.

9. Scala Cinema, Chillingham Road

When the Scala picture hall opened in 1913, at the corner of Tosson Terrace and Chillingham Road in a rapidly expanding residential area, it was one of 30 new cinemas built in Newcastle in the silent films era just before the First World War. The cinema was opened by a former sheriff of Newcastle, Alderman Arthur Scott (a great, great uncle of the author). At the ceremony he refuted the claim there were too many cinemas in the city and claimed there was still a strong demand for picture halls.

Percy L. Browne, a Newcastle architect, designed the building with 1,200 seats (later reduced to 1,051) at a cost of £7,000. It had a spacious tiled entrance with a marble staircase leading to the dress circle, red plush upholstery and a large stage with dressing rooms for artistes. The Scala faced financial difficulties during the 1930s, mainly due to new purpose-built cinemas, specifically designed to present talking films, appearing in Heaton. Despite this, the Scala survived for about 20 years showing revivals and B-features. The photograph is dated 1936.

The Scala closed in 1961 as a result of diminishing audiences and increased costs. A supermarket now covers the site.

10. Chillingham Road - Cartington Terrace junction

A 1979 photograph of the central part of Chillingham Road, near to its junction with Cartington Terrace.

The tall gabled building, left of centre, is a former retail branch of the Newcastle Co-operative Society that opened here in 1910. Some decorative plaster work inscribed '1910 NCSL' is visible on the upper part of the building. Today the building houses a pharmacy together with a post office around the corner in Cartington Terrace.

To the left of the Co-op building is the site of the former Scala cinema.

Most of the street names in this area are Northumbrian place names associated with Lord Armstrong of Cragside, who owned much of the land in this part of Heaton.

11. St Gabriel's Parish Hall, Cartington Terrace

Opened in 1925 at the corner of Chillingham Road and Cartington Terrace, this new parish hall for the church of St Gabriel's was built to cater for the various organisations that had outgrown their earlier home adjoining the church in Heaton Road.

Consisting of a large hall capable of seating 500 and several rooms for other activities, this sizable two-storied building was designed by J.W. Boyd to be 'fire resistant throughout'. Church activities were expected to meet the estimated total cost of £8,000.

This 1966 photograph was taken in Cartington Terrace looking towards Chillingham Road. St Gabriel's Children's Day Nursery now occupies the building.

12. Heaton Pool

When this pool opened in April 1925, along with a similar one at Walker, they were described in the press as 'Crystal clear swimming pools with attractively fitted slipper baths'. Slipper baths could be hired for single bathing and were partially covered and shaped like a slipper.

Designed by Mr A. W. Cross, a London architect, each pool measured 75ft x 35ft and contained 65,000 gallons of water. The cost of £42,000 for both pools was defended on the grounds that 'Newcastle was not extravagant' and that 'their baths and wash houses only cost 2d in the pound, this being half the cost in most other places'.

This photograph of Heaton Pool in Biddlestone Road in 1995 was taken just a few years before it closed to be replaced by the East End Pool, which opened near Shields Road in 2000. A doctor's surgery, opened in 2003, now occupies the site of the former pool.

13. North Heaton Council Schools

This 'plain and honest' public elementary school opened in North Heaton between Tosson Terrace and Trewhitt Road in 1904, four months ahead of schedule. It 'cost less than any other Board School built in the last ten years due to the omission of costly and useless ornamentation'. Designed by local architect S.D. Robins to cater for nearly 1,400 children, there was a mixed school and a smaller infant's school.

The mixed school was double storey with a central hall surrounded by seven classrooms on each floor to cater for a total of 952 pupils. The separate infants school was only single storey but again had a central hall and seven surrounding classrooms for 410 children.

At the opening ceremony, children from neighbouring Chillingham Road School sang the hymn *Strong Son of God*. The girls gave a display of club drill and the boys showed off their dumb bell routines.

This photograph, taken in November 1966, shows part of the mixed school from the Trewhitt Road entrance for girls –'GIRLS' is clearly visible on both gate pillars. Boys entered the school from Tosson Terrace where 'BOYS' is distinctly engraved on each gate pillar.

Following reorganisation in the 1950s, the school became North Heaton Secondary Modern and Technical Schools. It closed in the 1980s. Today these buildings house the Heaton Community Centre.

14. Iris Brickfield Community Park

Iris Brickfield Community Park lies between Rothbury Terrace (alongside the railway) and Whitefield Terrace in the north-eastern part of Heaton. Originally fields, some time before 1906 a clay pit with adjoining brickworks were created at a time of extensive house building in the vicinity. The site was close to the former Middle Pit, where spoil-heaps would probably have indicated that the clay beneath ground level was suitable for brick making. The Iris Brick Company, which operated the business, appears to have been part of a group. This photograph probably dates from around 1910.

J.W. Middlemiss

Index of roads and streets, people, places

Bold indicates an illustration.

Heaton Park Road South, 1938.